THE KNITTER'S COMPANION

VICKI SQUARE

INTERWEAVE PRESS

Design and production, Elizabeth R. Mrofka
Cover design, Signorella Graphic Arts
Illustration, Vicki Square

Text and illustration copyright 1996, Vicki Square

Interweave Press, Inc.
201 East Fourth Street
Loveland, Colorado 80537
USA

Printed in Singapore by Tien Wah Press

Library of Congress Cataloging-in-Publication Data

Square, Vicki, 1954–
    The knitter's companion / by Vicki Square.
      p. cm.
   Includes index.
   ISBN 1-883010-13-6
   1. Sweaters. 2. Knitting. I. Title.
  TT825.L714   1996
  746.43'2—dc20   95-38807
                                  CIP

First printing: IWP—10M:1295:TW   Second printing: IWP—7.5M:896:TW
Third printing: IWP—10M:197:TW   Fourth printing: IWP—10M:497:TW
Fifth printing: IWP—6M:298:TW   Sixth printing: IWP—20M:698:TW

PREFACE

For me, knitting is a creative endeavor. It goes beyond making a useful item to wear or use. In this age of advanced technology, I find unrestrained pleasure in being able to make something with my hands in the same way that someone did centuries ago.

Learning to knit is a process of perfecting and challenging. Give yourself the gift of pleasure in the process, and do not unwisely hope to be an expert in a few short lessons. Even if you've been knitting for a hundred years, there is always more to learn and experience. Try a technique you haven't used, or perfect one you're familiar with. Try a new fiber, or an old one in a new way. Make a tiny beaded bag on size 0000 needles, or a quick mohair afghan on size 17 needles.

This little book is meant to be your companion as you forge your knitting skills. Because it's small enough to fit into your knitting bag, the information will always be available. This book is not meant to be an all-inclusive volume; if it were, you would not be able to carry it with you. But it does cover the information, charts, and techniques that knitters most commonly need, and the "most used" and "best loved" finishing techniques. Those of you who knit beautifully and then put the pieces in the closet because your finishing techniques are lacking, take heart. Follow the drawings and practice the techniques. You can do it!

I've also included helpful preparatory information, for you cannot produce your best without adequate preparation. Beginning with the yarn and its care, through choosing gauge, style, and fit, to the finishing techniques, this book will help ensure a successful outcome.

Carry this little book with your knitting. My prayer is that it will help enhance your skills, and that it will be an encouraging companion in your growing experience as a knitter.

 Vicki Square

TABLE OF CONTENTS

In Preparation

Supplies and Notions 6
Yarn Structure 7
Yarn Sizes 8
Yarn Label Symbols 10
Handwashing 12
Formula for
    Interchanging Yarns 14
Yardage Estimates for Typical
    Weights and Styles 16
Taking Body Measurements . . 18
Body Measurement Tables . . . 20
Sweater Ease Allowances 25
Weights and Lengths 26
Knitting Needle Conversion
    Chart 27
Crochet Hook Conversion
    Charts 28
Abbreviations 29

The Basics

Gauge 32
Knit Stitch—Continental 34
Purl Stitch—Continental 35
Knit Stitch—English 36
Purl Stitch—English 37
Measuring the Knitting 38
Slipping Stitches 39
Yarnovers 40

Casting On

Introduction 41
Slip Knot 42
Cable Cast On 43
Long-Tail Cast On 44
Invisible or Open Cast On . . . 46

Joining Yarns

Joining at the Side Edge 47
Overlapping the Old
    and New Yarn 48
Splicing 49

Increases

Introduction 50
Bar Increase 51
Raised Increase 52
Make One, Right Slant 54
Make One, Left Slant 55
Double Increase 56
Open Work Increase 58

Decreases

Knit Two Together 59
Slip Slip Knit 60
Slip Knit Pass 61
Purl Two Together 62
Purl Two Together Through
    Back Loops 62
Slip Purl Pass 63
Double Decreases 63
Vertical Double Decrease 64

Binding off

Basic Bind Off 65
Sloped or Bias Bind Off. 66
Binding Off Together 67

Blocking

Introduction 68
Wet Blocking 69
Steam Blocking 69

Seaming

Introduction 70
How to Begin. 71
Invisible Weaving on Stockinette
    Stitch—One-Half Stitch Seam
    Allowance 72
Invisible Weaving on Stockinette
    Stitch—One-Stitch Seam
    Allowance 73
Invisible Weaving on Reverse
    Stockinette Stitch 74
Invisible Weaving on
    Single (1 × 1) Rib 75

Invisible Weaving on
    Double (2 × 2) Rib. 76
Invisible Weaving on
    Garter Stitch 77
Seaming with Slip
    Stitch Crochet 78
Backstitch Seaming. 79
Invisible Horizontal Seam . . . 80
Invisible Vertical to Horizontal
    Seam. 81
Kitchener Stitch 82
Applying a Vertical Border of
    Single (1 × 1) Rib 84

Hems and Hemming

Turning Rows. 85
Hem Stitches 86

Borders and Edges

Single (1 × 1) Rib 88
Double (2 × 2) Rib. 88
Garter Stitch. 89
Seed Stitch. 89
Crocheted Edges. 89

Buttonholes

Eyelet Buttonhole 91
One-Row Buttonhole 92

Other Information

Shortrowing 93
Picking Up Stitches. 96
Color Knitting. 98
Using Double-Pointed
    Needles 102
Duplicate Stitch 104
Correcting Errors 105

A Final Word

. . . . 110

IN PREPARATION

Supplies and Notions

Knitting bag, or bags!

Knitting needles—Ideally you'll have circular, single- and double-pointed straight needles in every size. Most knitters acquire needles as needed.

Stitch gauge

Needle gauge

Stitch markers

Stitch holders

Point protectors

Cable needles—Small, medium, and large to use with fine to bulky projects.

Crochet hooks—Various sizes for correcting mistakes and working edges.

Knitting pins—2-inch (5-cm)- long steel pins with colored heads to pin pieces together for seaming.

Large-eye tapestry needle

Scissors

Tape measure

Storage bags in various sizes for holding stitch markers, holders, point protectors, pins, tapestry needles, cable needles, crochet hooks, scissors, tape measure, and other small items that tend to get lost (soft cloth zipper bags are great).

Notebook

Sticky notes—Good for quick notations and marking your place in a pattern.

Magnet board—indispensable for tracking each row when following a complex pattern or following a graph.

Nail file—Handy for honing off a rough fingernail that catches yarn.

Yarn Structure

All yarn is made of spun fiber, whether the fibers are natural such as wool, cotton, or silk, or synthetic such as acrylic, or a blend. Spinning twists the fibers together to make a continuous, strong yarn. A single strand of spun fiber is called a singles. Plying two, three, or four singles together makes two-ply, three-ply, or four-ply yarn, and so on. But the number of plies does not determine the weight of the yarn—there are single-strand bulky yarns, as well as four-ply fingering yarns.

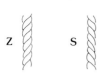

Twisted yarn spirals in either the "Z" twist (in which the twists run upward to the right) which is considered standard, or the "S" twist (in which the twists run upward to the left). In evenly textured yarns, the strands all have the same thickness. Novelty yarns combine strands of different thicknesses or textures.

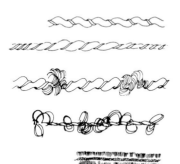

Spiral. A thin yarn spun around a thick yarn.

Slub. A single strand which is alternately thick and thin, plied with either a smooth or slubbed strand.

Nub. Two strands plied so that one overwinds at certain intervals producing bumps.

Bouclé. Two strands plied at different tensions producing loops which are held in place with a thin binder thread.

Chenille. Two thin threads tightly plied around a short velvety pile.

Yarn Sizes

Yarns fall into six categories:

Fingering-weight or baby yarn is best suited for fitted clothing such as socks or gloves, and baby clothing. Use knitting needles ranging in size from 0 to 3, and work 28 or more stitches to 4 inches (10 cm).

Sport-weight yarn is about twice as thick as fingering yarn, with an extremely wide variety of uses, from heavier socks to lighter pullovers or cardigans. Use knitting needles ranging in size from 4 to 6, and work about 20 to 24 stitches to 4 inches (10 cm).

DK, or double knitting yarn, is the British designation for a yarn slightly thicker than sport but slightly finer than American worsted. This weight yarn is appropriate for anything that sport or worsted yarn is used for. Use knitting needles ranging in size from 4 to 6, and work about 22 stitches to 4 inches (10 cm).

Worsted-weight yarn is useful for everything from garments to afghans to accessories. Use knitting needles ranging in size from 6 to 9, and work 16 to 20 stitches to 4 inches (10 cm).

Chunky yarn is heavier than worsted and is useful for outdoor sweaters and accessories, and lightweight jackets. Use knitting needles ranging in size from 9 to $10^{1}/_2$, and work 14 to 15 stitches to 4 inches (10 cm).

Bulky yarn is any yarn that is heavier than chunky. Knit heavy sweaters, coats, and afghans with this weight of yarn. Use knitting needles size 10 and larger, and work 8 to 12 stitches to 4 inches (10 cm).

Although I have listed the common uses for each yarn type, don't let this stifle your imagination. Adopt a "no-rules" attitude to create the look you want. For example, a beautiful airy, lacy shawl can be knit with fingering yarn on size $10^{1}/_2$ needles.

Yarn Label Symbols

Needles and hooks

 Manufacturer's suggested knitting needle size in US and/or metric sizes.

 Manufacturer's suggested crochet hook in US and/or metric sizes.

Gauge or tension

Manufacturer's suggested gauge with the suggested needle size. It will usually read so many stitches and so many rows will equal 4" × 4" or 10 cm × 10 cm.

Washing

Note: Tub and temperature diagrams may not always mean machine washable.

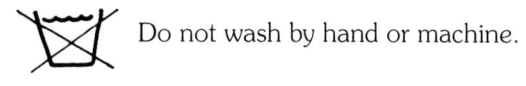 Do not wash by hand or machine.

Handwashing

 Handwash in lukewarm water only.

 Handwash in warm water temperature indicated.

Machine washing

 Machine wash in warm water at temperature indicated, cool rinse, short spin.

 Machine wash in warm water at temperature indicated.

Bleaching

  No bleaching.

 Chlorine bleach permitted.

Pressing

 Do not press.

 Press with a cool iron.

 Press with a warm iron.

 Press with a hot iron.

Dry cleaning

 Do not dry clean.

 May be dry cleaned with fluoro-carbon or petroleum-based solvents only.

 May be dry cleaned with perchlorethylene or fluorocarbon or petroleum-based solvents.

 May be dry cleaned with all solvents.

Note: Check with your dry cleaner as to which solvents are used.

Handwashing

After you have spent countless hours knitting and finishing a garment, you should not be casual about its care. You can extend the life of a garment indefinitely by practicing good handwashing techniques. Always use pure soap flakes or special wool detergent. Wash and rinse gently but thoroughly in warm (not hot or cold) water.

Test for colorfastness by dipping a corner of a garment in warm soapy water, then gently pressing out the liquid onto a clean white cloth. If any color stains the cloth, wash the garment in cold water; otherwise, use warm water. Colors that bleed badly can be "set" with a rinse of one-quarter cup vinegar to one gallon water, prior to each washing. Do not leave garments to soak for long periods, particularly if they are intensely- or multi-colored, as the risk of color bleeding increases.

Fill a basin with warm water of the appropriate temperature. Add the pure soap flakes or wool detergent, and use your hands to work up a lather. Place the garment in the basin and gently squeeze the suds into it. Avoid rubbing the knitted fabric, or felting (shrinkage and matting of the fibers) may occur.

Rinsing

To rinse, remove the garment from the basin, drain the water, fill the basin again with warm clear rinse water, and add the garment. Gently squeeze the garment in the water to remove the suds. Repeat this procedure until the rinse water is clear. Use your hands to press as much water out of the garment as possible, roll it up in a thick towel, and again press out as much water as possible. Repeat this with a second towel if necessary. Be careful not to wring the garment at any stage of this process.

Drying

To dry the garment, arrange it to the shape you desire on a sweater drying rack or flat surface covered with a dry towel, away from direct sun or heat.

Store garments flat. Storage on a hanger will cause the knitted fabric to sag and distort the shape of the garment.

Formula for Interchanging Yarns

Yarns of similar weight and similar texture can generally be interchanged effectively.

The number of balls required × yards (or meters) per ball = total number of yards (or meters) needed.

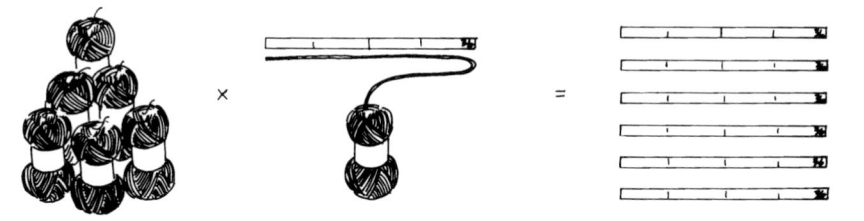

The total number of yards (or meters) needed divided by the number of yards (or meters) in one ball of substitute yarn = number of balls needed of substituted yarn.

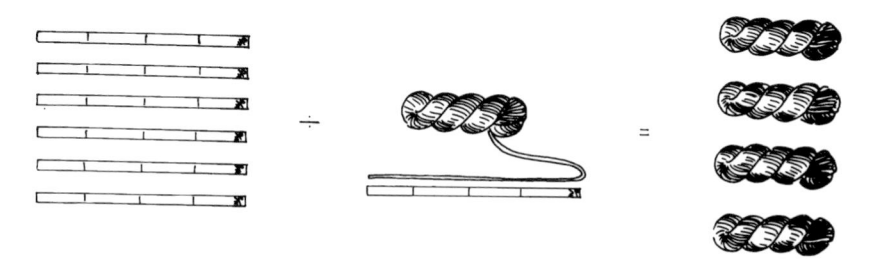

For example, if 12 balls are required of the suggested yarn, and each ball contains 145 yards (130 meters), then the total number of yards needed is

12 balls × 145 yards (130 meters) per ball = 1740 total yards (1560 meters).

If you want to substitute a yarn that has 163 yards (146 meters) per ball, then you need

1740 total yards (1560 meters) ÷ 163 yards (146 meters) per ball = 10.67 balls.

Because you must buy full balls of yarn (and because it's always a good idea to have a little extra yarn) you will need to buy 11 balls of the substitute yarn.

Working with the total yardage (or number of meters) is much more accurate than interchanging ounces or grams. There can be a large range in length between balls of two different yarns of the same weight. This variety is determined by the fiber type, number of plies, and tightness of the twist. If you have only the weight to guide you, consider purchasing two more balls than your accounting would indicate to allow for possible differences in yardage. Most yarn shops will refund the purchase price of unopened balls of yarn within a few months. But if you're like me, you'll want to collect left-over balls of yarn and then get wildly creative when your stash is full.

Yardage Estimates for Typical Weights and Styles

The following guidelines are for the amounts of yarn needed for a basic pullover or cardigan in a variety of sizes and yarn weights. These estimates are for smooth yarns and plain or lightly textured knitting. Keep in mind that heavily textured patterns such as Aran or all-over cables, or oversized looks can easily require additional yarn (400–600 yards; 375–550 meters). When you knit with two or more colors, your total yardage will be greater to account for the yarns being carried across the back of the work. Estimate generously, and if you have leftovers . . . well, they're a designer's best friend!

Babies   12–18 months (for a pullover or cardigan)
600–700 yards (550–650 meters) fingering-weight yarn

Toddlers   2–6 years (for a pullover or cardigan)
800–1000 yards (750–950 meters) sport-weight yarn
600–800 yards (550–750 meters) worsted-weight yarn
550–650 yards (500–600 meters) bulky yarn

Children   6–12 years (for a pullover or cardigan)
1000–1500 yards (950–1400 meters) sport-weight yarn
900–1200 yards (850–1100 meters) worsted-weight yarn
700–1000 yards (650–950 meters) bulky yarn

Misses   sizes 32–40
For a regular, comfortable ease pullover
1500–1700 yards (1400–1600 meters) fingering-weight yarn
1400–1600 yards (1300–1500 meters) sport-weight yarn
1100–1400 yards (1000–1300 meters) worsted-weight yarn
1000 yards (950 meters) bulky yarn

For a longer, loosely fitting, or oversized pullover
1500–1900 yards (1400–1750 meters) sport-weight yarn
1300–1500 yards (1200–1400 meters) worsted-weight yarn
900–1200 yards (850–1100 meters) bulky yarn

Men   sizes 36–48
For a regular, comfortable ease pullover
1700–2100 yards (1600–1950 meters) sport-weight yarn
1500–1700 yards (1400–1600 meters) worsted-weight yarn
1300–1500 yards (1200–1400 meters) bulky yarn

For a longer, loosely fitting, or oversized pullover
2000–2400 yards (1850–2200 meters) sport-weight yarn
1800–2000 yards (1650–1850 meters) worsted-weight yarn
1500–1700 yards (1400–1550 meters) bulky yarn

Taking Body Measurements

Accurate measurements will help you determine the size garment to knit. But keep in mind that you'll want to add some ease (see the chart on page 25 for suggested amounts). Some of these measurements are difficult to take by yourself—get someone to help you so that the measurements are accurate. If you have a sweater that fits just the way you want, you're in luck. Simply measure the sweater and knit yours to match.

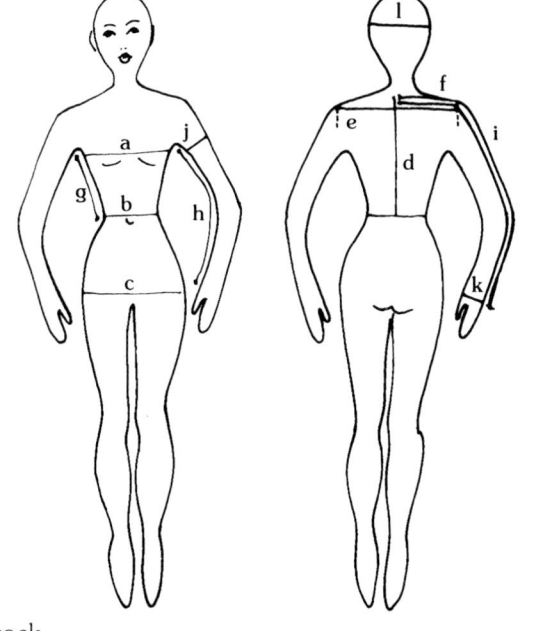

Bust/chest (a). Measure around the fullest part. Make sure the tape measure doesn't slip down in the back.

Waist (b). Measure the smallest part where a belt would be worn.

Hip (c). Measure the fullest part, generally 9 to 10 inches (23 to 25.5 cm) below the waist. Make sure that the tape measure doesn't slip down in the back.

Back length (d). Measure from the prominent neck bone to the waist. It helps to tie a piece of yarn around the waist for accuracy—a common mistake is to measure too far into the small of the back.

18

Back width (e). Measure across the back from one shoulder bone to the other. (This is slightly different than taking a back width for sewing.)

One shoulder (f). Measure from the center back neck bone to the edge of the shoulder bone.

Waist to underarm (g). Tie a strand of yarn around the waist and measure from this waist marker to about one inch below the underarm crease. This measurement will help you determine where to begin the armhole shaping.

Wrist to underarm (h). Measure from the wrist bone along the inside of the arm to about 1 (2.5 cm) inch below the armhole crease. This determines where to begin sleeve cap shaping for a set-in sleeve.

Center back neck to wrist (i). Holding the arm with the elbow slightly bent out to the side, measure from the center back neck bone, across the shoulder bone, and down across the elbow to the wrist bone. This measurement minus the "one shoulder" measurement will give the sleeve length.

Upper arm circumference (j). Measure the fullest part of the upper arm.

Wrist circumference (k). Measure around the wrist bone just above the hand.

Head circumference (l). A head circumference is helpful in determining the size of a crew neck opening, and of course, for hats.

Body Measurement Tables

The "average" body measurements given here are based on the National Bureau of Standards. These measurements will help you plan garment sizes, and are especially helpful when you are knitting for gift giving. Be sure to add ease to the measurements to make the garment fit comfortably. For example, to size a sweater for a friend who wears a Misses size 12, consult the body measurement table for Misses sizes on page 22 and then use the Sweater Ease Allowances chart on page 25 to determine how much ease to add to achieve the fit you want. The measurements are given in inches with centimeters in parentheses.

Babies

Size	Newborn	Six month	12 months
Chest	to 18 (45.5)	to 20 (51)	to 22 (56)
Waist	18 (45.5)	19 (48)	20 (51)
Hip	19 (48)	20 (51)	21 (53.5)
Back length	6 $\frac{1}{8}$ (15.5)	6 $\frac{7}{8}$ (17.5)	7 $\frac{1}{2}$ (19)
Back width	7 $\frac{1}{4}$ (18.5)	7 $\frac{3}{4}$ (19.5)	8 $\frac{1}{4}$ (21)
One Shoulder	2 (5)	2 $\frac{1}{4}$ (5.5)	2 $\frac{1}{2}$ (6.5)
Waist to underarm	3 (7.5)	3 $\frac{3}{8}$ (8.5)	3 $\frac{3}{4}$ (9.5)
Wrist to underarm	6 (15.5)	6 $\frac{1}{2}$ (16.5)	7 $\frac{1}{2}$ (19)
Armhole depth	3 $\frac{1}{4}$ (8)	3 $\frac{1}{2}$ (9)	3 $\frac{3}{4}$ (9.5)
Upper arm circumference	6 $\frac{1}{2}$ (16.5)	7 (18)	7 $\frac{1}{4}$ (18.5)
Wrist circumference	5 (12.5)	5 $\frac{1}{8}$ (13)	5 $\frac{1}{8}$ (13)
Head circumference	15 (38)	15 (38)	16 (40.5)

Children

Size	2	4	6	8	10	12
Chest	21(53.5)	23 (58.5)	25 (63.5)	27 (68.5)	28½ (72.5)	30 (76)
Waist	20 (51)	21 (53.5)	22 (56)	23 (58.5)	24 (61)	25 (63.5)
Hip	22 (56)	24 (61)	26 (66)	28 (71)	30 (76)	32 (81.5)
Back length	8½ (21.5)	9½ (24)	10½ (26.5)	12½ (31.5)	14 (35.5)	15 (38)
Back width	8¾ (22)	9½ (24)	10¼ (26)	11 (28)	11½ (29)	12 (30.5)
One Shoulder	2¾ (7)	3 (7.5)	3⅜ (8.5)	3⅝ (9)	3¾ (9.5)	4 (10)
Waist to underarm	4 (10)	4 (10)	4½ (11)	6¼ (16)	7½ (19)	8 (20.5)
Wrist to underarm	8½ (21.5)	10½ (26.5)	11½ (29)	12½ (31.5)	13½ (34.5)	15 (38)
Armhole depth	4¼ (11)	5½ (14)	6 (15.5)	6¼ (16)	6½ (16.5)	7 (17.5)
Upper arm circumference	7½ (19)	8 (20.5)	8½ (21.5)	9 (23)	9⅜ (24)	9¾ (24.5)
Wrist circumference	5¼ (13.5)	5½ (14)	5½ (14)	5¾ (14.5)	6 (15)	6 (15)

(Measurements are in inches with centimeters in parentheses.)

Misses

Size	6	8	10	12	14	16	18
Bust	30½ (77.5)	31½ (80)	32½ (82.5)	34 (86.5)	36 (91.5)	38 (96.5)	40 (101.5)
Waist	23 (58.5)	24 (61)	25 (63.5)	26½ (67)	28 (71)	30 (76)	32 (81.5)
Hip	32½ (82.5)	33½ (85)	34½ (87.5)	36 (91.5)	38 (96.5)	40 (101.5)	42 (106.5)
Back length	15½ (39.5)	15¾ (40)	16 (40.5)	16¼ (41)	16½ (42)	16¾ (42.5)	17 (43)
Back width	13½ (34)	13½ (34)	14 (35.5)	14½ (37)	15 (38)	15½ (39.5)	16 (40.5)
One Shoulder	4¾ (12)	4¾ (12)	5 (12.5)	5 (12.5)	5 (12.5)	5¼ (13.5)	5¼ (13.5)
Waist to underarm	8½ (21.5)	8¾ (22)	8¾ (22)	8¾ (22)	8¾ (22)	8¾ (22)	9 (23)
Wrist to underarm	16¾ (42.5)	16¾ (42.5)	17 (43)	17½ (44.5)	17¾ (45)	18 (45.5)	18¼ (46.5)
Armhole depth	7 (18)	7 (18)	7½ (19)	7½ (19)	7½ (19)	8 (20.5)	8 (20.5)
Upper arm circumference	9¾ (24.5)	9¾ (24.5)	10¼ (26)	10½ (26.5)	11 (28)	11½ (29)	12 (30.5)
Wrist circumference	6 (15)	6 (15)	6¼ (16)	6¼ (16)	6½ (16.5)	6½ (16.5)	6½ (16.5)

(Measurements are in inches with centimeters in parentheses.)

Women

Size	38	40	42	44	46	48	50
Bust	42 (106.5)	44 (112)	46 (117)	48 (122)	50 (127)	52 (132)	54 (137)
Waist	35 (89)	37 (94)	39 (99)	$41\frac{1}{2}$ (105.5)	44 (112)	$46\frac{1}{2}$ (118)	49 (124.5)
Hip	44 (112)	46 (117)	48 (122)	50 (127)	52 (132)	54 (137)	56 (142)
Back length	$17\frac{1}{4}$ (44)	$17\frac{3}{8}$ (44)	$17\frac{1}{2}$ (44.5)	$17\frac{5}{8}$ (44.5)	$17\frac{3}{4}$ (45)	$17\frac{7}{8}$ (45.5)	18 (45.5)
Back width	$16\frac{1}{2}$ (42)	17 (43)	$17\frac{1}{2}$ (44.5)	18 (45.5)	18 (45.5)	$18\frac{1}{2}$ (47)	$18\frac{1}{2}$ (47)
One Shoulder	$5\frac{1}{2}$ (14)	$5\frac{1}{2}$ (14)	$5\frac{3}{4}$ (14.5)	$5\frac{3}{4}$ (14.5)	6 (15.5)	$6\frac{1}{4}$ (16)	$6\frac{1}{4}$ (16)
Waist to underarm	9 (23)	9 (23)	$9\frac{1}{4}$ (23.5)	$9\frac{1}{4}$ (23.5)	$9\frac{3}{8}$ (24)	$9\frac{1}{2}$ (24)	$9\frac{3}{4}$ (24.5)
Wrist to underarm	$18\frac{1}{4}$ (46)	$18\frac{1}{4}$ (46)	$18\frac{1}{4}$ (46)	$18\frac{1}{4}$ (46)	$18\frac{1}{4}$ (46)	$18\frac{1}{4}$ (46)	$18\frac{1}{4}$ (46)
Armhole depth	$8\frac{1}{4}$ (21)	$8\frac{1}{4}$ (21)	$8\frac{1}{4}$ (21)	$8\frac{1}{2}$ (21.5)	$8\frac{1}{2}$ (21.5)	$8\frac{3}{4}$ (22)	$8\frac{3}{4}$ (22)
Upper arm circumference	13 (33)	$13\frac{1}{2}$ (34.5)	14 (35.5)	15 (38)	$15\frac{3}{4}$ (40)	$16\frac{1}{2}$ (42)	17 (43)
Wrist circumference	$6\frac{3}{4}$ (17)	7 (17.5)	$7\frac{1}{4}$ (18.5)	$7\frac{1}{2}$ (19)	$7\frac{3}{4}$ (19.5)	8 (20.5)	8 (20.5)

(Measurements are in inches with centimeters in parentheses.)

Men

Size	34	36	38	40	42	44	46	48
Chest	34 (86.5)	36 (91.5)	38 (96.5)	40 (102)	42 (107)	44 (112)	46 (117)	48 (122)
Waist	28 (71)	30 (76)	32 (81)	34 (86.5)	36 (91.5)	39 (99)	42 (107)	44 (112)
Hip	35 (89)	37 (94)	39 (99)	41 (104)	43 (109)	45 (114)	47 (119.5)	49 (124.5)
Back length	22 (56)	23 (58.5)	24 (61)	25 (63.5)	26 (66)	26½ (67.5)	27½ (70)	28½ (72.5)
Back width	15½ (39.5)	16 (40.5)	16½ (42)	17 (43)	17½ (44.5)	18 (45.5)	18½ (47)	19 (48)
One Shoulder	5 (12.5)	5¼ (13)	5½ (14)	5½ (14)	5½ (14)	6 (15)	6 (15)	6 (15)
Wrist to underarm	17½ (44.5)	18 (46)	18½ (47)	19 (48)	19½ (49.5)	20 (51)	20 (51)	20½ (52)
Waist to underarm	14 (35.5)	14½ (37)	15 (38)	15½ (39.5)	16 (40.5)	16 (40.5)	16½ (42)	17 (43)
Armhole depth	8 (20)	8½ (21.5)	9 (23)	9½ (24)	10 (25.5)	10½ (26.5)	11 (28)	11½ (29)
Upper arm circumference	13 (33)	13½ (34.5)	14 (35.5)	14½ (37)	15½ (39.5)	16 (40.5)	16½ (42)	17 (43)
Wrist circumference	6¼ (16)	6½ (16.5)	6¾ (17)	7 (18)	7¼ (18.5)	7½ (19)	7¾ (19.5)	8 (20.5)

(measurements are in inches with centimeters in parentheses.)

Sweater Ease Allowances

(Measurements are in inches with centimeters in parentheses.)

SIZE	FINISHED BUST/CHEST MEASUREMENT				
Bust/chest	Body hugging minus 5–10%	Close fitting plus 0–5%	Normal fitting plus 7–10%	Loose fitting plus12–15%	Oversized plus 16–20%
31–33 (79-84)	30 (76)	32 (81)	34 (86.5)	36 (91.5)	more than 36 (91.5)
33–35 (84-89)	32 (81)	34 (86.5)	36 (91.5)	38 (96.5)	more than 38 (96.5)
35–37 (89-94)	34 (86.5)	36 (91.5)	38 (96.5)	40 (101.5)	more than 40 (101.5)
37–39 (94-99)	36 (91.5)	38 (96.5)	40 (101.5)	42 (106.5)	more than 42 (106.5)
39–41 (99-104)	38 (96.5)	40 (101.5)	42 (106.5)	44 (112)	more than 44 (112)
41–43 (104-109)	40 (101.5)	42 (106.5)	44 (112)	46 (117)	more than 46 (117)

Weights and Lengths

CONVERSIONS

Ounces	=	Grams × 0.035
Grams	=	Ounces × 28.57
Inches	=	Centimeters × 0.3937
Yards	=	Meters × 0.9144
Centimeters	=	Inches × 2.54
Meters	=	Yards × 1.0936

WEIGHTS

3/4 oz	=	21.5	grams
1 oz	=	28.5	grams
$1\frac{1}{2}$ oz	=	43	grams
$1\frac{3}{4}$ oz	=	50	grams
2 oz	=	57	grams
$3\frac{1}{2}$ oz	=	100	grams

LENGTHS

Yards to Meters		Meters to Yards	
5	4.5	5	5.5
50	46	50	54.5
100	91	100	109.5
150	137	150	164
200	183	200	218.5
300	274	300	328
400	365	400	437.5

Knitting Needle Conversion Chart

US	METRIC	UK	US	METRIC	UK
0	2 mm	14	8	5 mm	6
1	$2^1/_4$ mm	13	9	$5^1/_2$ mm	5
	$2^1/_2$ mm		10	6 mm	4
2	$2^3/_4$ mm	12	$10^1/_2$	$6^1/_2$ mm	3
	3 mm	11		7 mm	2
3	$3^1/_4$ mm	10		$7^1/_2$ mm	1
4	$3^1/_2$ mm		11	8 mm	0
5	$3^3/_4$ mm	9	13	9 mm	00
6	4 mm	8	15	10 mm	000
7	$4^1/_2$ mm	7			

Crochet Hook Conversion Charts

ALUMINUM, PLASTIC, BONE, WOOD					
US	**METRIC**	**UK**	**US**	**METRIC**	**UK**
	2 mm	14		5 mm	
B/1	2.25 mm	13	I/9	5.5 mm	5
	2.5 mm	12	J/10	6 mm	4
C/2	2.75 mm		K/10½	6.5 mm	3
	3 mm	11		7 mm	2
D/3	3.25 mm	10		7.5 mm	
E/4	3.5 mm	9	L/11	8 mm	
F/5	3.75 mm	8	M/13	9 mm	
	4 mm		N/15	10 mm	
G/6	4.25 mm	7	P/16	15 mm	
	4.5 mm		Q	16 mm	
H/8	4.75 mm	6	S	19 mm	

STEEL		
US	**METRIC**	**UK**
00	3.5 mm	
0	3.25 mm	0
1	2.75 mm	1
2	2.25 mm	1½
3	2.1 mm	2
4	2 mm	2½
5	1.9 mm	3
6	1.8 mm	3½
7	1.65 mm	4
8	1.5 mm	4½
9	1.4 mm	5
10	1.3 mm	5½
11	1.1 mm	6
12	1 mm	6½
13	0.85 mm	7
14	0.75 mm	

ABBREVIATIONS

A
alt . . . . alternate
approx . . . . . . approximately

B
b. . . . . bobble
bc . . . . back cross
beg . beginning; begin; begins
bet . . . . between
bo . . . . bind off
but . . . . buttonhole

C
cab . . . . cable
cc. . . . . contrasting color
ch. . . . . chain
cm . . . . centimeter(s)
cn. . . . . cable needle
co . . . . cast on
col. . . . . color
cont . . . . continue

cr l. . . . . cross left
cr r . . . . cross right

D
dbl . . . . double
dc . . . . double crochet
dec . . . . decrease; decreasing
decs . . . . decreases
diag . . . . diagonal
diam . . . . diameter
dk . . . . double knitting
dpn. . . double-pointed needle
dtr . . . . double treble crochet

E
e. . . . . every
eor . . . . every other row
eon. . . . . end of needle

F
fc . . . . front cross
fin. . . . . finished

foll. . . . . following

G
g . . . . grams
grp . . . . group(s)
g st . . . . garter stitch
hdc . . . . half double crochet
hk. . . . . hook
htr . . . . half treble

I
in(s) . . . . inch(es)
inc . . . . increase; increasing
incl . . . . including
inst. . . . . instructions

K
k . . . . knit
kbl (k tbl) . . . . . . knit through
back of loop
kfb . . . . . knit into the front
and back of a stitch

k2tog . . . . . knit two together
kwise . . . . knitwise

L

l . . . . left
lc . . . . left cross
lh . . . . left hand
ln . . . . left needle
lp(s) . . . . loop(s)
lt . . . . left twist

M

m . . . . meter(s)
mb . . . . make bobble
mc . . . . main color
med . . . . medium
mm . . . . millimeters
m1 . . . . make one
mult . . . . multiple

N

no . . . . number

O

opp . . . . opposite

oz . . . . ounce

P

p . . . . purl
patt(s) . . . . pattern(s)
p-b . . . . . purl into the stitch
in the row below
pfb . . . . . . purl into the front
and back of next stitch
pm . . . . place marker
pnso . . . pass next stitch over
psso . . . . pass slip stitch over
p tbl . . . . purl through
back of loop
p2tog . . . . purl two
stitches together
p2tog-b . . . . purl two stitches
together through
back of loop
pwise . . . . purlwise

R

rc . . . . right cross

rem . . . . remaining
rep . . . . repeat
rev st st . . . . reverse
stockinette stitch
rh . . . . right hand
rib . . . . ribbing
rnd(s) . . . . round(s)
rs . . . . right side
rt . . . . right twist

S

sc . . . . single crochet
sel . . . . selvedge
sk . . . . skip
skn . . . . skein
skp . . . . . slip one, knit one,
pass slip stitch
over (one stitch decreased)
sl . . . . slip
sl st . . . . slip stitch
sp . . . . space

ssk . . . . slip, slip, knit
(one stitch decreased)
st(s) . . . . stitch(es)
st st . . . . . . stockinette stitch
T
tbl . . . . through back of loop
tch . . . . turning chain
tog . . . . together
tr . . . . treble crochet
W
won . . . . . . wool over needle
wrn . . . . . wool round needle
ws . . . . wrong side
wyib . . . . . . with yarn in back
wyif . . . . . . with yarn in front
V
yb . . . . yarn back
yf . . . . yarn forward
yfon . . . . yarn forward
and over needle

yfrn . . . . yarn forward
and round needle
yo . . . . yarn over
yon . . . . . . yarn over needle
yo2 . . . . yarn over twice
yrn . . . . . . yarn round needle
ytb . . . . yarn to back
ytf . . . . yarn to front
Z
zip . . . . zipper

---

* repeat starting or stopping point (i.e., repeat from *)
* * repeat all instructions between asterisks
( ) alternate measurements and/or instructions
[ ] alternate measurements and/or instructions; also used to indicate instructions that are to be worked as a group a specified number of times

THE BASICS

Gauge

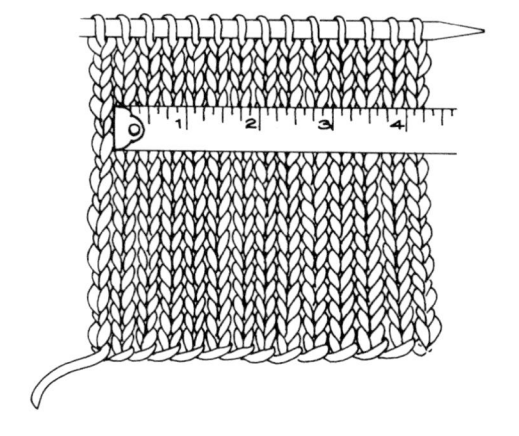

Gauge, or tension, is the most critical factor in obtaining an accurate fit. All patterns are based on a specific number of stitches and rows per inch. If your knitting doesn't match that specification, your garment stands little chance of fitting properly.

To determine gauge, knit a sample swatch with the yarn and needles you intend to use for the garment. Always knit a swatch at least 4 inches (10 cm) wide and 4 inches (10 cm) long, even if the pattern you plan to follow specifies a gauge of a certain number of stitches over 1 inch (or cm). Because the stitches at the edges of the knitting tend to be somewhat misshapen, you'll want to measure at least two stitches in from the selvedge edges of the swatch. Therefore, cast on at least 4 more stitches than needed to make 4 inches (10 cm) of knitting width. Work the pattern stitch specified to check the gauge; if no pattern is given, work the swatch in stockinette stitch. If the pattern is complex, such as Aran or lace, you should work a larger swatch, perhaps 8 inches (20 cm) square.

To measure the swatch, lay the swatch flat, place a tape measure or ruler parallel to a row of stitches, and count the number of stitches (including fractions of stitches) that are in 4 inches (10 cm). This is your stitch gauge per 4 inches (10 cm). Compare this gauge to that specified by the pattern. If your swatch has too few stitches per 4 inches (10 cm), your work is too loose and you should try again with smaller needles. If your swatch has too many stitches, your work is too tight and you should try again with larger needles.

When your gauge matches that specified by the pattern, you are ready to begin knitting. The gauge swatch may be saved or reused. You can bind off the stitches and use the swatch to test the washability of the yarn, put it in a notebook with other swatches for future reference, use it with other swatches to make a patchwork afghan, or use it for technique practice. If you want to reuse the yarn in the gauge swatch, ravel the swatch and wrap the yarn around the outside of the ball. Begin your knitting with another ball to give the raveled yarn time to relax.

It is important that you test the gauge and that you strive for accuracy. When I was young, being quite the knitter that I was, I thought I was "beyond gauge". I merrily dove into a project, enjoyed the process immensely, but ended up with a garment wide enough to fit a football player, and long enough to fit a toddler. I ate humble pie that day, and forevermore have enjoyed knitting gauge swatches.

Knit Stitch—Continental Method

I wholeheartedly recommend using the Continental method, that is, holding the working yarn in your left hand, for its speed and ease of execution.

Hold the needle with the cast-on stitches in your left hand.

1. Hold the working yarn in back of the needle, over your left index finger, and in your palm against the needle (or around your little finger) for tension.

2. Insert the right needle into the first stitch, from front to back. Catch the working yarn by moving the right needle over and behind it.

3. Pull the working yarn through the stitch to the front, forming a new stitch on the right needle and slipping the stitch off the left needle.

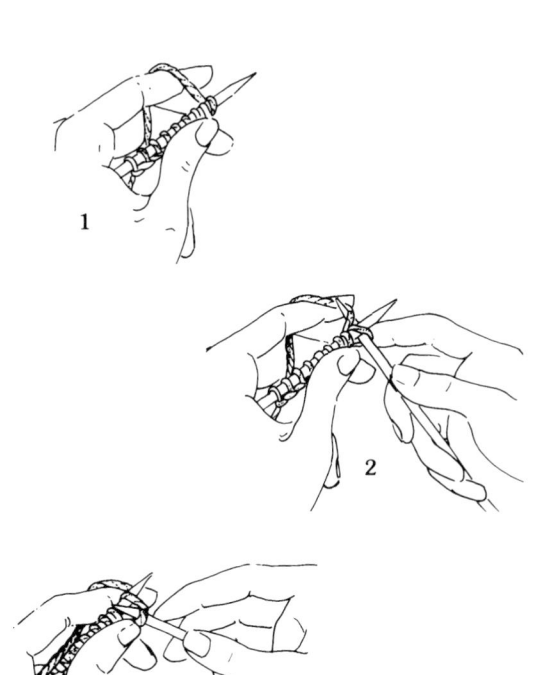

Purl Stitch—Continental Method

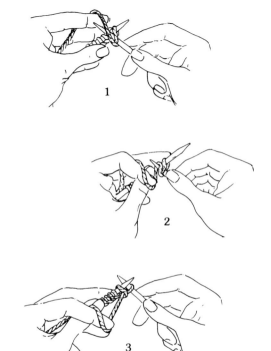

The Continental method of purling allows for smooth and fast knitting, particularly when switching the working yarn from front to back to change from knit to purl, as for ribbing and other textural stitches.

Hold the needle with the cast-on stitches in your left hand. Hold the working yarn in your left hand, over your index finger, and in your palm against the needle (or around your little finger) for tension.

1. Holding the working yarn in front of the needle, insert the right needle into the first stitch, from back to front.

2. With your left index finger, lay the working yarn over the right needle from front to back, and then down between needles.

3. Leverage the right needle to the back, through the cast-on stitch. Leaving the newly formed stitch on the right needle, slip the stitch off of the left needle.

Knit Stitch—English Method

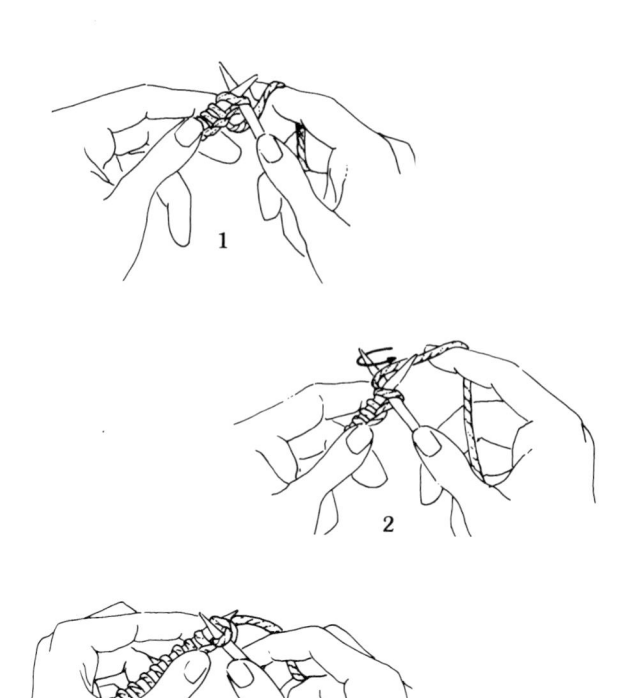

In the English method, the working yarn is held in the right hand, and is thrown or passed around the needle.

Hold the needle with the cast-on stitches in your left hand. Hold the working yarn in your right hand, over your index finger and wound around your little finger for tension.

1. With the working yarn held in back, insert the right needle into the first stitch on the left needle, from front to back.

2. Use your right hand to wrap the yarn under and around the needle.

3. Pull the wrapped needle back through the cast-on stitch to the front, forming a new stitch on the right needle and slipping the stitch off the left needle.

Purl Stitch— English Method

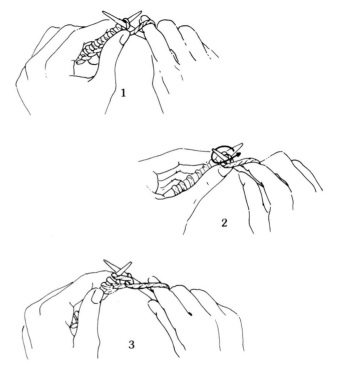

H old the needle with the cast-on stitches in your left hand. Hold the working yarn in your right hand, over your right index finger and wound around your right little finger for tension.

1. Holding the working yarn in front of the needle, insert the right needle into the first stitch, back to front.

2. Wrap or "throw" the working yarn behind and around the right needle in a counterclockwise motion.

3. Leverage the right needle back through the stitch. Leaving the newly formed stitch on the right needle, slip the stitch off the left needle.

Measuring the Knitting

To measure knitting length, as in ribbing, garment, or sleeve length, lay the work on a flat surface and, without stretching it, measure the center of the piece from the bottom edge to the lower edge of the knitting needle.

To measure an area that has been shaped, such as an armhole or a sleeve, measure on the straight of grain (perpendicular to the bottom edge). For example, measure an armhole by laying a ruler or other straight edge horizontally across the garment, even with the first row of bound-off stitches. From that straight edge, measure vertically to the lower edge of the knitting needle. On a sleeve, measure along the center of the sleeve. **Do not** follow along the slanted, shaped side edge! Erroneous measuring will result in sleeves that are too short, armholes that are too shallow, and an overall appearance of being squeezed into your sweater. Not an attractive sight. . . .

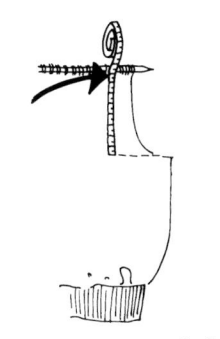

measuring an armhole

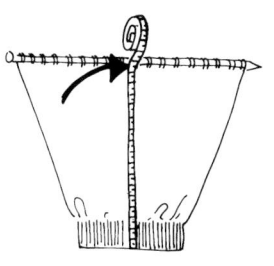

measuring a sleeve

Slipping Stitches

To slip a stitch, simply pass it from one needle to the other without knitting or purling it. Beginners commonly try to outwit this little move, expecting it to be more than it is. Look for slipped stitches in some decrease methods, decorative stitches, and on selvedges.

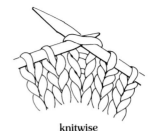

knitwise

To slip knitwise, insert the right needle into the first stitch on the left needle as if you were going to knit it, then slip it off the left needle and onto the right.

To slip a stitch purlwise, insert the right needle into the first stitch on the left needle as if you were going to purl it, then slip it off the left needle and onto the right.

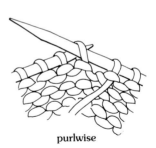

purlwise

Yarnovers

Yarnovers produce open increases. You'll avoid confusion if you think of them as being worked in two steps. The first step is to lay the yarn from front to back over the needle. The second step is to place the working yarn in front of or behind the needle in preparation for the next stitch.

Prepare for the first step as follows: if the working yarn proceeds from a knit stitch on the right needle, bring the yarn forward under the needle and then lay it over the needle, front to back. If the working yarn proceeds from a purl stitch, the yarn is already in the front and you can simply lay it over the needle, front to back.

Prepare for the second step as follows: if the next stitch to be worked will be knit, leave the working yarn in back of the needles. If the next stitch will be purled, bring the working yarn to the front of the needles.

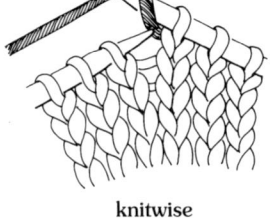

knitwise

purlwise

CASTING ON

The cast-on row is the foundation for the knitting. There are a variety of ways to cast on; the most common are outlined here. But before you begin, note the following preparation tips which will help ensure the most uniform and professional looking edge possible.

The ribbing in most sweater styles is knit on 10%–20% fewer stitches than used in the body of the sweater, and it is commonly worked on needles two or even three sizes smaller than used for the body. Within these guidelines, the greater the difference in the number of stitches and sizes of needles used for the ribbing and body, the tighter the ribbing will be. Determine the style of fit you prefer, and then adjust the number of stitches and needle size accordingly.

If you tend to cast on tightly, use a needle one, two, or even three sizes larger than the recommended needle, and then remember to switch to the correct needle size when you begin knitting.

When you prepare to cast on, allow for an 18-inch (45-cm) tail of yarn that will be used to sew the seam. (The fewer ends to be worked in when finishing, the better!) To keep the tail out of the way while you knit, knit a few inches, thread the tail in a tapestry needle, and loop it through the knitting several times.

Slip Knot

Do you remember the "magic" knot you learned as a child? With just a snap of the wrist the knot would disappear. Almost all cast-on methods begin with this knot.

With the tail end of the yarn in your palm, wrap the working yarn around your index and middle fingers, and lay the working yarn across the tail end, forming an "×". Spread your fingers slightly and push the working yarn through your fingers from the back of your hand. Pull this loop up slightly while holding the tail end of the yarn to form a knot. Place the loop onto the knitting needle and pull working yarn to adjust the tension.

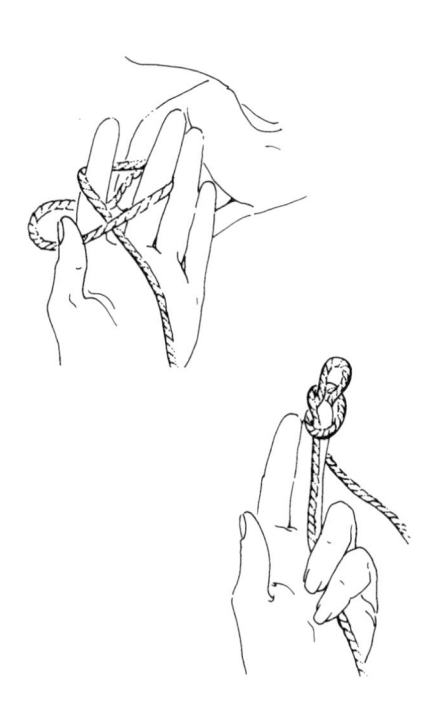

Cable Cast On

The cable cast on is wonderful for its reversibility. It produces a smooth, twisted cable effect on the lower edge, viewed from either side. Because it is not very elastic, this cast on is best suited for pieces that do not require an elastic edge, such as cropped sweaters or jackets that have no ribbing, afghans, and scarves.

Begin by making a slip knot (leaving an 18-inch (45-cm) tail for seaming) and placing it on a knitting needle held in your left hand. Insert the right needle into the slip knot as if to knit. Pull a loop forward and place it on the left needle.

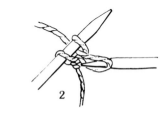

1. Insert the right needle between the two stitches, wrap it as if to knit.

2. Pull the loop forward.

3. Place the loop on the left needle. Continue in this fashion, working between the last two stitches on the needle, until you have the desired number of stitches.

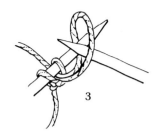

Tip: If you insert the right needle between the two stitches **before** you pull the working yarn for tension, you will have no trouble inserting the needle and your tension will be more uniform.

Long-Tail Cast On

The long-tail cast on is easily the most common cast-on method and is used by beginners as well as long-time knitters. It creates a firm but elastic edge. The stitches produced by this cast on are smooth on the front side and have bumps similar to purl stitches on the back side. I like to have the smooth sides of the cast-on stitches on the right side of my garments, so when I use this cast on, I make my first row of knitting a wrong-side row.

To begin, make a slip knot, leaving a long tail. A simple way to figure out how long to make the tail is to wrap the yarn around the needle, one wrap per stitch to be cast on. You can simplify this by wrapping the needle just 20 times to determine the length needed for 20 stitches and then multiply this length by the number of times 20 goes into the total number of stitches needed. Of course, it's always a good idea to leave a little extra for seaming.

Example: 100 stitches needed divided by 20 wraps = 5 lengths, plus a little.

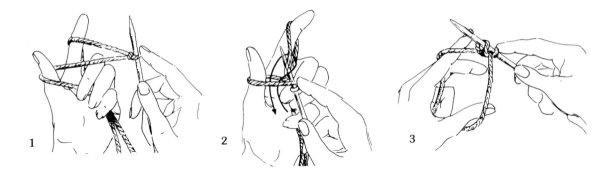

1. Leaving the determined length for a tail, make a slip knot with the yarn and place it on a knitting needle held in your right hand. Let the tail end of yarn lay over your left thumb and the working end over your left index finger. Turn your hand and needle to a vertical position, catching the yarn in your palm with your remaining fingers.

2. Insert the needle upward into the loop that is on your thumb. Catch the working yarn on your index finger by moving the needle over the yarn, and then press the needle downward back through the loop on your thumb.

3. Remove your thumb from the loop and then adjust the tension of the resulting stitch by pulling on the needle gently while repositioning your thumb under the tail end of the yarn in preparation for the next stitch. You should not have to let go of the yarn secured in your palm. Repeat until you have the desired number of stitches.

Invisible or Open Cast On

Use this temporary cast-on method when you need access to the bottom loops of the cast-on stitches for picking up to knit or graft (as in ribbings, borders, and peplums) or hem (as in the lower edges of jackets or skirts).

To begin, knot the working yarn to a length (a yard is usually sufficient) of contrasting waste yarn. Use your right thumb to hold the knot against a knitting needle in your right hand.

1. Hold the yarns in your left hand with the working yarn over the needle and the waste yarn over your thumb.

2. Work as for the long-tail method, inserting the right needle up into the waste yarn on your thumb, around the working yarn on your index finger, and down through waste-yarn loop on your thumb.

3. Remove your thumb from the loop and pull the needle gently to adjust the tension. Repeat until you have the desired number of stitches.

When you are ready to pick up to knit, graft, or hem the stitches, use fine pointed scissors to clip the waste yarn out of each stitch, and place each resulting loop on a needle.

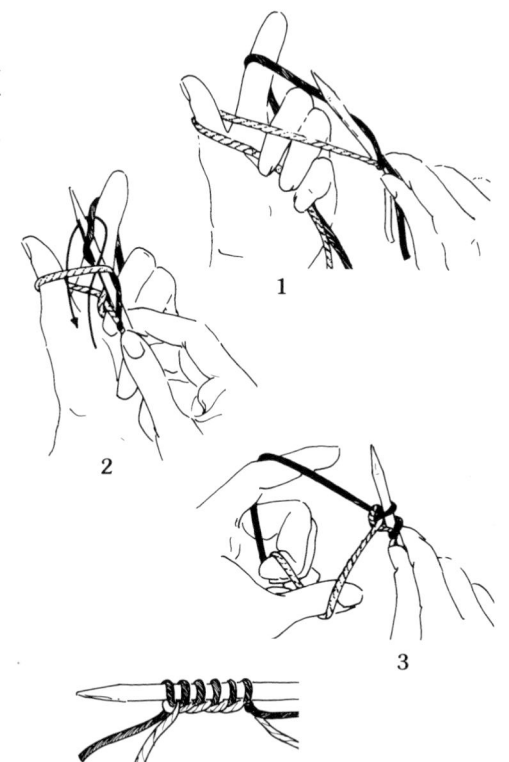

JOINING YARNS

There are many ways to start new balls of yarn, and just as many opinions about which is correct. I believe that each method has its advantages.

Joining at the Side Edge

The easiest way to join a new ball of yarn at the side edge is to simply drop the old ball and begin to knit with the new, leaving the ends to be worked in later.

This method has the advantages of uninterrupted rows, no double thickness of yarn, and no knot at the side seam. It is especially well suited for bulky yarns. The disadvantage is that the work feels loose and unstable and the ends of yarn have to be pulled to maintain tension of the end stitches.

Another method is to firmly tie a new ball onto the old ball using the first half of a square knot. Then slide the half-knot up to just behind the stitch on the needle. Then continue knitting with the new ball of yarn.

This method has the advantage of uninterrupted knitted rows and feels quite stable where the new ball begins. The disadvantage is that there is the bulk of the half-knot in the seam. This method works on virtually all yarns, but is especially useful for slippery yarns such as cottons, and any pattern of lace or open work.

joining with a square knot

Overlapping the Old and New Yarn

Use this joining method in an inconspicuous place, such as 1 to 2 inches (2.5 to 5 cm) in from the side edge or in a textured area. This method is well suited for wools, synthetics, blends of any kind, and novelty yarns, as long as they are worsted weight or finer. When worked with nonelastic yarns such as cotton and ribbon yarn, this join may be visible from the right side.

Overlapping the end of the old yarn with the beginning of the new, work two stitches with the two strands held together. Then drop the old and continue with the new ball. On the next row, knit the double-strand stitches as single stitches.

During finishing, secure the two loose ends by needle weaving them diagonally into the wrong side of the knitted fabric. Weaving the ends in horizontally or vertically can create a visible ridge on the right side.

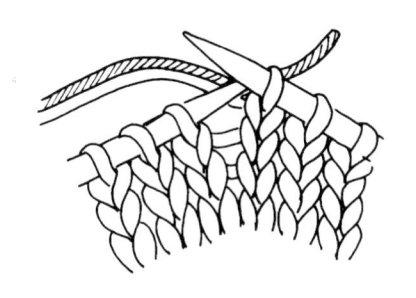

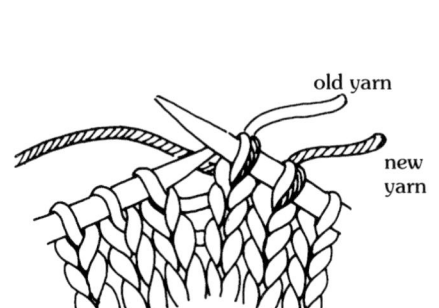

old yarn

new yarn

Splicing

To splice, untwist approximately 4 inches (10 cm) from the ends of both the old and the new yarns. Take half of the plies from each and then twist them together. Continue your knitting with the twisted yarn, working in the loose ends later.

Although more tedious than the other two methods mentioned, splicing forms an invisible join that can be used anywhere on a row. It secures the two yarns together without adding bulk or knots.

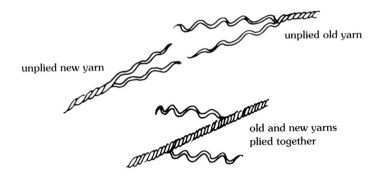

unplied old yarn

unplied new yarn

old and new yarns
plied together

INCREASES

By adding stitches, one or two at a time, you can shape a piece of knitting to make it wider. Increases can be subtle or they can be quite visible and used decoratively. It is good to know several methods so you can choose the type that is most appropriate for your project.

Increases are usually made one or two stitches in from the edge of the knitting so that they don't interfere with the edge stitch used for seaming. Most patterns specify that increases be made on the right side of the work. This makes it easier to keep track of when to increase and allows you to see the increases that have been worked. If you have trouble keeping track of the increases, or if for some reason you must increase on a wrong-side row, try slipping an open marker into each increase as it is completed. Then simply count the markers. Alternately, use a stitch counter or make a pencil mark on a piece of paper each time you make an increase.

Bar Increase

This type of increase forms a purl bar visible on the knit side of the knitting, hence its name. A bar increase is nice and tight, and leaves no hole. It is especially good for increasing on the last row of ribbing, just before the body of a sweater begins because its stability helps the ribbing maintain its shape (instead of fanning out as may happen with other increase methods).

Working from the knit side, simply knit a stitch in the usual way, but don't slip it from the left needle. Then knit into the same stitch again, but through the back of the loop, and then slip the stitch from the needle. You will have made two stitches from one.

To work this increase from the purl side, purl a stitch in the usual way without slipping it from the left needle. Then purl into the same stitch again, but through the back of the loop, and then slip the stitch from the needle.

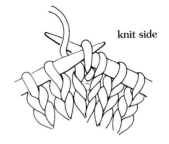

knit side

purl side

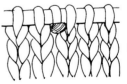

finished look

Raised Increase

This increase is nearly invisible and works well for all the basic shaping in the body and sleeves of a garment.

To work a raised increase from the knit side, insert the right needle into the back of the loop of the stitch below. (To see the back of the loop, tilt the knitting slightly toward you.) Knit this stitch, and then knit the stitch on the needle.

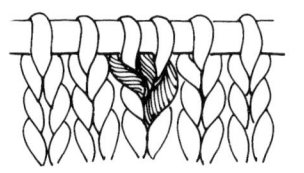

finished look

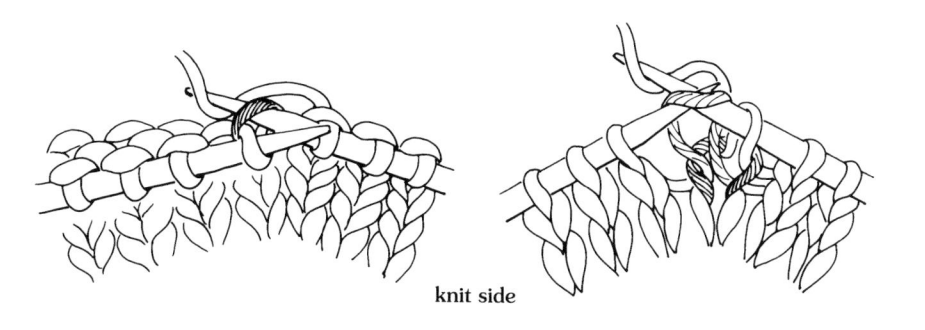

knit side

To work this increase from the purl side, insert the right needle from the top into the purl stitch below the needle. Purl this stitch, then purl the one on the needle. You may have trouble purling into the stitch below, particularly if you are using a short circular needle. If this is the case, try lifting the lower purl stitch onto the left needle so that you can use the needle to hold it as you purl it.

A common mistake is to forget to work the stitch on the needle as part of the increase after working the stitch below. If you don't work both, you won't have increased any stitches.

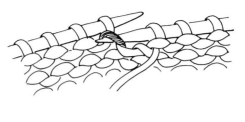

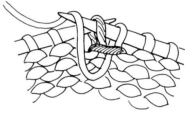

purl side

Make One, Right Slant

This subtle increase slants to the right on the knit side. It may be used in conjunction with the make one, left slant (page 55) for shaping symmetry. For this increase, you make a stitch out of the horizontal "ladder" that forms between every two stitches.

To work this increase on the knit side, insert the left needle from back to front under the ladder. Knit this lifted strand through the front to twist the stitch to the right.

To work this increase on the purl side, insert the left needle from back to front under the ladder. Purl this lifted strand through the front to twist the stitch to the right.

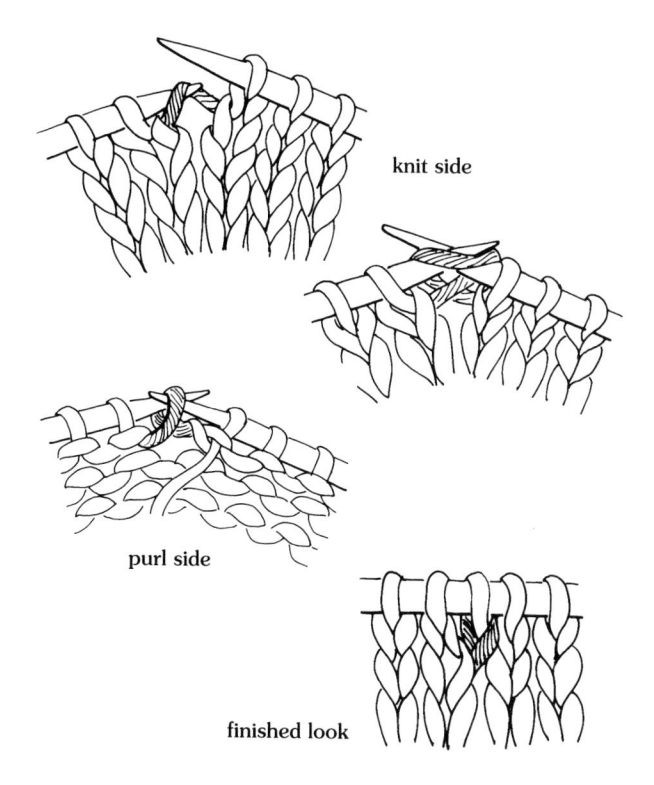

knit side

purl side

finished look

Make One, Left Slant

This subtle left-slanting increase is a mirror image of the make one, right slant on the previous page.

To work this increase on the knit side, insert the left needle from front to back under the horizontal "ladder" between the two needles. Knit this lifted strand through the back to twist the stitch to the left.

To work this increase on the purl side, insert the left needle from front to back under the ladder. Purl this lifted strand through the back to twist the stitch to the left.

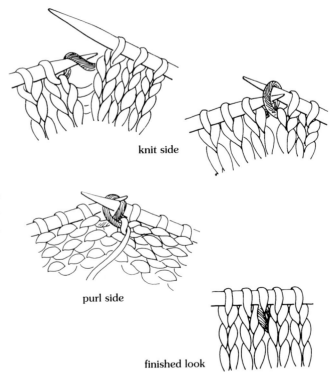

knit side

purl side

finished look

Double Increase

A double increase causes the work to widen at twice the rate as a single increase. It is generally worked on the right side of the knitting by working two increases, one on either side of a plain stitch, called the axis stitch. Double increases are generally worked in the middle of a piece, not at the sides. They are used in garments worked from the neck down and for mitering corners.

To work a double increase, increase immediately before the axis stitch, work the axis stitch, and then increase immediately following the axis stitch. The type of increase to use depends on the look you want. For example, a double make-one increase (page 57) might be used when mitering a corner where only a subtle effect is needed. A double openwork increase (page 57) may be used as a dressier textural design for raglan shoulder shaping when knitting from the neck down.

Double bar increase. Work a bar increase into the stitch preceding the axis stitch and another bar increase into the axis stitch.

double bar increase

Double raised increase. Knit into the stitch directly below the axis stitch by catching the purl loop behind the stitch, then knit through back of the loop of the axis stitch (to avoid a hole), and finally, knit again into the stitch below by catching the purl loop behind the stitch. This will make two increases in the axis stitch and will look somewhat like a raised rope cable.

Double make-one increase. Use the ladders immediately before and after the axis stitch. The increase will appear symmetrical if you use a make-one, right slant on one side of the axis stitch and a make-one, left slant on the left side, or vice versa.

Double openwork increase. Yarn over immediately before and after the axis stitch.

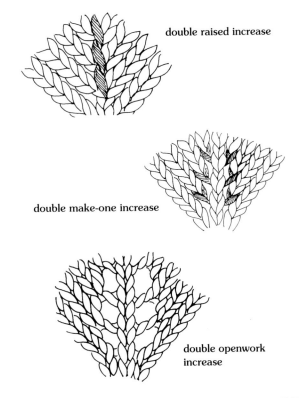

double raised increase

double make-one increase

double openwork increase

Openwork Increase

This decorative increase may be used with lacy patterns or on garments that need a pronounced raglan shaping, as in baby clothes or dressy cardigan jackets. A yarn over (yo) creates an extra stitch which is then worked as a regular stitch on the following row.

On a knit row, the working yarn is in the back. To yarn over, bring the yarn between the needles to the front, then over the right needle and again to back. This will form a new stitch on the right needle and will position the yarn for the next knit stitch.

On a purl row, the working yarn is in the front. Yarn over by laying the yarn over the top of the right needle and then bringing it to the front between the needles. This will form a new stitch on the right needle and will position the yarn for the next purl stitch.

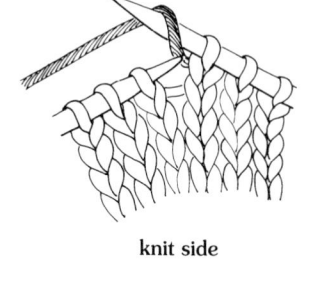

knit side

purl side

DECREASES

Decreasing subtracts stitches, one or two at a time, to make a knitted piece narrower. As with increases, there are several methods to choose from. The most popular methods are the knit two together (k2tog), slip slip knit (ssk), and slip knit pass (skp) decreases.

The k2tog and ssk decreases are essentially mirror images of each other, one slanting right and the other slanting left. They are generally used in tandem for symmetrical shapings; for example, the armhole shaping on a sweater or instep shaping on a sock. In general, use the ssk decrease at the beginning of a row and the k2tog decrease at the end of a row.

Knit Two Together (k2tog)

This is a subtle right-slanting decrease that is worked on a knit row. Insert the right needle into two stitches (at the same time) knitwise, and knit them as one.

Slip Slip Knit (ssk)

This is my favorite left-slanting decrease. It is worked on a knit row, and is more subtle than the slip knit pass decrease shown on the next page.

To work this decrease, slip two stitches knitwise, one at a time, onto the right needle. Then insert the point of left needle into the front of the two slipped stitches to hold them in place while you knit them together through the back of the loops with the right needle.

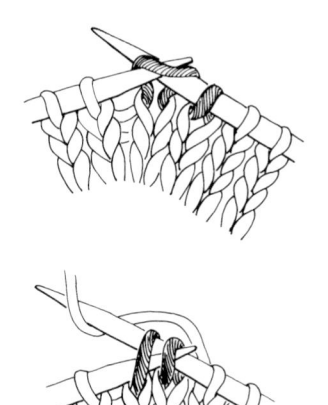

Slip Knit Pass (skp)

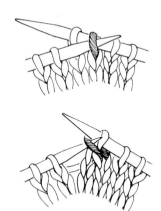

This decrease is worked on a knit row and produces a fairly pronounced left-slanting decrease. It is best used in lace patterns or with other textural stitches where a visible decrease is a necessary part of the finished look.

To work this decrease, slip one stitch knitwise, knit the next stitch, and then use the point of the left needle to pass the slipped stitch over the knit stitch and off the right needle. To minimize the prominence of the decrease, avoid stretching the stitch as you pass it over.

For exaggerated shaping, such as in knitting chevron shapes, this decrease can be combined with k2tog (page 59) to make a double decrease. Work the double decrease by slipping one stitch knitwise, k2tog, and then passing the slipped stitch over.

Purl Two Together (p2tog)

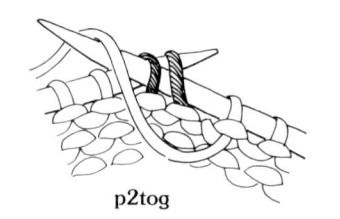

This decrease is worked on a purl row and causes a right-slanting decrease on the knit side. To work this decrease, insert the right needle into two stitches (at the same time) purlwise, and then purl them as one.

p2tog

Purl Two Together Through Back Loops (p2tog tbl)

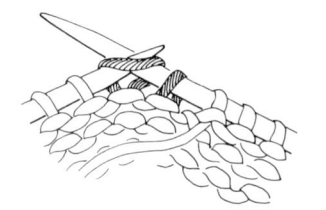

This decrease is worked on a purl row and causes a left-slanting decrease on the knit side.

p2tog tbl

To work this decrease, slip two stitches knitwise, one at a time, to the right needle. Return these two stitches to the left needle, keeping them twisted. Then purl these two stitches together as one through the back loops.

Slip Purl Pass (spp)

This decrease is worked on a purl row and causes a right-slanting decrease on the knit side. It forms a mirror image of the p2tog tbl decrease (page 62).

To work this decrease, slip a stitch purlwise, purl the next stitch, and then pass the slipped stitch over the purled stitch and off the right needle.

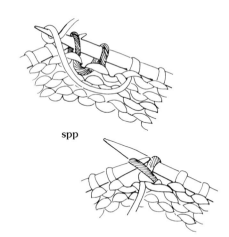

spp

Double Decrease

For a more dramatic reduction of stitches, work two decreases, one on each side of a center axis stitch. Double decreases are generally worked on right-side rows.

For the best results, work a left-slanted decrease over the two stitches immediately preceding the axis stitch, work the axis stitch, and then work a right-slanted decrease over the two stitches immediately following the axis stitch (i.e., ssk, knit 1, k2tog).

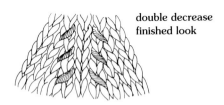

**double decrease
finished look**

Vertical Double Decrease

This double decrease creates a neat, slightly raised axis stitch.

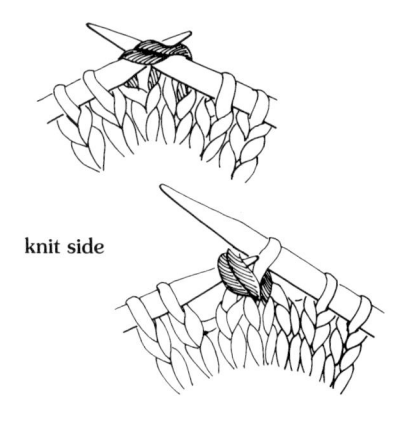

On a knit row, insert the right needle into two stitches (at the same time) knitwise and slip them to the right needle. Knit the next stitch, and then with the left needle, pass both slipped stitches over the knitted stitch and off the right needle.

knit side

On a purl row, with yarn in front, slip the next two stitches, one at a time, knitwise. Purl the next stitch, and with the left needle, pass the two slipped stitches over the purled stitch and off the right needle.

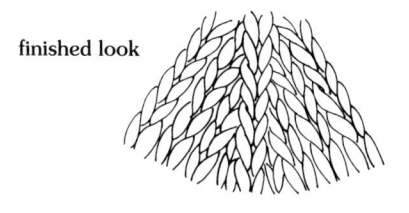

finished look

BINDING OFF

Binding off secures the last row of the knitting so that it will not ravel. Binding off is also used for shaping when more than two stitches need to be eliminated at one time, such as at armholes or necklines. The bound-off edge may be the finished edge of a border, seamed, or may need overcasting, as in buttonholes.

Many knitters tend to bind off too tightly, causing puckers and undue stress on the bound-off edge. You can prevent this problem by binding off with a knitting needle one or two sizes larger. The three most common methods are described here.

Basic Bind Off

This is the most common and easiest bind-off method. To bind off on a knit row, first knit two stitches, then *with the two stitches on the right needle, pass the right stitch over the left and off the end of the needle. Knit the next stitch. Repeat from * until the required number of stitches have been bound off.

The process is the same for binding off on the purl side, with the exception that you'll purl instead of knit. For ribbing, or any other pattern stitch, bind off in pattern, that is, knit the knit stitches and purl the purl stitches, always passing the right stitch over the left and off the end of the needle. If you bind off all of the stitches on the needle, cut the working yarn and pull the cut end through the last stitch to secure it.

Sloped or Bias Bind Off

This method creates a smoothly shaped edge without the stairstep effect created by a series of basic bind offs. On the row preceding the bind-off row, do not work the last stitch. Turn work. There will be one stitch on the right needle. Place the working yarn in back and slip the first stitch on the left needle purlwise. Pass the unworked end stitch over the slipped stitch and off the end of the needle. This will bind off one stitch. Knit the next stitch and continue binding off as for the basic bind-off method (page 65).

Loose Loop Alert: When all of the stitches on the needle are bound off, the last stitch can be quite loose. To tighten and neaten this stitch, work it with the stitch in the row below it: insert the right needle from the back into the stitch below the last stitch, lift this stitch and place it onto the left needle, then knit the stitch below and the last stitch together. Bind off the last stitch on the right needle, cut the yarn, and pull the cut end through last stitch to secure it.

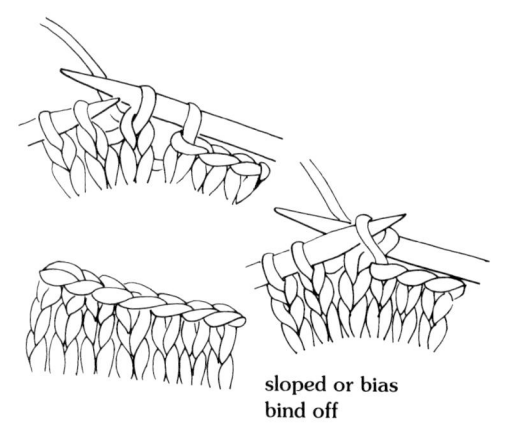

sloped or bias bind off

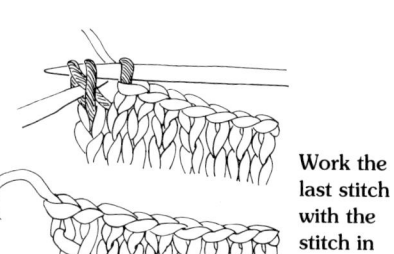

Work the last stitch with the stitch in the row below it.

Binding Off Together

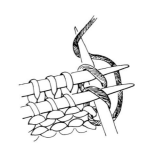

This superb technique is the perfect finish for shortrowing (see page 93) or unshaped shoulder seams in which the stitches are still on the needles. There are many advantages to this technique: it is efficient to bind off two edges simultaneously; it produces a seam that is smooth and flat with very little bulk; and the bound-off stitches help to stabilize a shoulder seam that might otherwise stretch out (such as one that had been grafted).

To work this bind off, there must be the same number of stitches on each piece. With the two pieces still on knitting needles, place them right sides together with the needles parallel. Insert a third needle, one or two sizes larger, knitwise into the first stitch on both needles and knit these together as one. There will be one stitch on the right needle. Repeat. There will be two stitches on the right needle. Pass the right stitch over the left and off the end of the right needle. Continue to knit together the first stitch on both left needles and then pass the right stitch over the left and off the right needle until only one stitch remains on the left needle. To prevent this stitch from forming a loose bind-off loop (see page 66), knit into the stitch below the last stitch on both the front and back needles, and slip the stitches off the needles as you do so. There will be two stitches on the right needle. Pass the right stitch over the left as before, cut the yarn, and secure the last stitch by pulling the tail of yarn through it.

BLOCKING

Blocking is the process of wetting or steaming the knitted pieces to even out the lines of the stitches and the yarn fibers. For best results, block the pieces before you sew them together.

The bands around most knitting yarns give instructions for blocking. Read these instructions before you begin. In general, cotton, linen, wool, and wool-like fibers (alpaca, camel hair, cashmere) can be either steam pressed or wet blocked. Mohair, angora, and wool blends should only be wet blocked, as should synthetics. Do not block lurex or highly textured novelty yarns.

Blocking requires a flat surface larger than the largest knitted piece. Block on an out-of-the-way place on the carpet or make a special padded surface for this purpose: Layer a particle board with heavy batting or foam 1/4 to 1/2 inch (0.5 to 1 cm) thick, and a sturdy surface fabric, such as canvas duck. Wrap the surface fabric to the back, and use a staple gun to attach it to the wood.

Use long straight pins, such as quilting pins, to pin the pieces to the blocking surface. First pin the length of a piece, then the width, and finally the curves and/or corners, measuring carefully at every step to ensure that it matches the dimensions given in the pattern. Place pins every few inches to prevent the piece from contracting as it dries. If you block on a very large surface such as the carpet, you may pin the pieces next to one another, lining up the selvedges that will be seamed to make sure that the seams will be even.

Wet Blocking

Moisten the pieces with water, pin them to the blocking surface, and allow them to air dry. You can use a spray bottle to moisten them or roll the knitted peices up in a large bath or beach towel which has been run through a rinse/spin cycle in a washing machine; place the roll in a plastic bag, and leave overnight. (Use two towels if the project is large.) The pieces will then be uniformly damp and ready to be pinned to the blocking surface. This method is safe for all types of yarns.

Steam Blocking

Hold an iron set on the steam setting 1/2 inch (1 cm) above the knitted surface and direct the steam over the entire surface, **except** the ribbing. You can get similar results by placing wet cheesecloth on top of the knitted surface and touching it lightly with a dry iron. Lift and set the iron down gently. Do not use a forward or sideways pushing motion. Leave the pieces pinned until they are dry.

Never steam-block ribbing that you want to remain elastic, as in the waist and cuff area. Once blocked, ribbing will remain stretched out. (However, you should block ribbing along a front cardigan border to flatten it and prevent it from pulling.)

If you sew, you know to "press as you go". So it is with knitting—seams should be "pressed" as soon as they are sewn. This does not mean that you should use a steam iron to smash the life out of the yarn in the seam area, but it does mean that you should wet the seam on the inside of the garment using steam or a spray bottle (according to the yarn type) and gently finger press the seam to reduce the bulk. This also serves to "set" the seaming yarn and prevents ends from working their way out.

SEAMING

Seaming is a very important step, second only to knitting quality, in giving a professional look to a garment. Practice these methods on knitting samples until you have flawless results to prevent stunning work from being relegated to the closet, never to see the light of day.

Seams should be sewn with the same yarn that was used to knit the garment unless the yarn is unplied or nubby. (Unplied yarn will be too weak and nubby yarn will be difficult to sew with.) If the garment was knit with an unplied or nubby yarn, sew the seams with a flat, firm yarn in a matching color.

To begin seaming, pin blocked pieces together for placement, easing in any fullness. The most common sequence of construction is to sew one or both shoulder seams, work the neckband (then sew the other shoulder seam, if necessary), sew the sleeves into the sweater body, and finish by sewing the side and sleeve seams. Take care to seam with even tension, pulling firmly, but not so tightly as to cause puckers. I like to block each seam after it is sewn by steaming or spraying it with a fine mist of water and pressing it with my fingers to reduce the bulk (see page 69). After all of the seams have been sewn, turn the garment inside out and work in all loose ends of yarn.

How to Begin

The join between the knitted pieces should be smooth along the cast-on edge. For the best results, use the tail from the cast-on row to start the seam. (If there is no tail, begin the seam with a new strand, leaving a 6-inch (15-cm) tail to be worked in after the seam is sewn). Thread the tail of yarn onto a tapestry needle and, with right sides facing you, insert the needle front to back just above the cast-on edge at the corner stitch of the piece without the tail, and then insert the needle from back to front into the piece with the tail, so that the yarn travels in a circle. Pull securely on the yarn to close the gap and make the bottom edge a smooth line with no indentations between pieces. Then use one of the seaming techniques on the following pages.

Invisible Weaving on Stockinette Stitch
One-Half Stitch Seam Allowance

This seam for stockinette stitch produces little bulk—it merges only half a stitch from each side. Less bulk allows more natural drape of the knitted fabric at the seam. Use this method for vertical seams such as sleeve and side seams. This technique works best on sport-weight or thicker yarns.

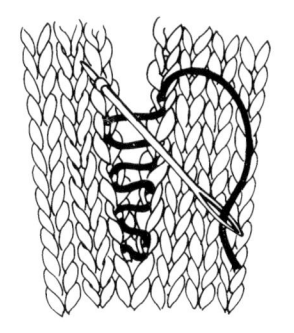

Work this seam from the right side of the knitting, placing the pieces to be seamed on a table, right sides up. Begin at the lower edge and work upward, row by row. Note that the edge stitches of stockinette stitch are misshapen. A large, loose stitch alternates every other row with a smaller, tighter stitch. At the base of the V-shaped tighter stitch is a horizontal bar. Insert a threaded tapestry needle under this bar, first on one side of the seam, and then under a corresponding bar on the opposite side. Continue alternating from side to side, pulling the yarn in the direction of the seam, not outward toward your body, to prevent the bar from stretching and pulling to the front.

When the seam is complete, turn the work to the wrong side. Whipstitch (see page 87) once over the seam allowance to secure the seam, and then weave the tail end down through the seam allowance for 2 inches (5 cm).

Invisible Weaving on Stockinette Stitch
One-Stitch Seam Allowance

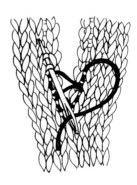

This technique is the best choice for stockinette stitch vertical seams, such as sleeve and side seams, on garments worked in fingering-weight yarn; sport-weight and heavier yarns will produce a slightly bulky seam allowance.

Work this seam from the right side of the knitting, placing the pieces to be seamed on a table, right sides up. Begin at the lower edge and work upward, row by row. Insert a threaded tapestry needle under two horizontal bars between the first and second stitches in from the edge on one side of the seam, and then under two corresponding bars on the opposite side. Continue alternating from side to side, pulling the yarn in the direction of the seam, not outward toward your body, to prevent the bars from stretching to the front.

When the seam is complete, turn the work to the wrong side. Whipstitch (see page 87) once over the seam allowance to secure the seam, and then weave the tail end down through seam allowance for 2 inches (5 cm).

Invisible Weaving on Reverse Stockinette Stitch

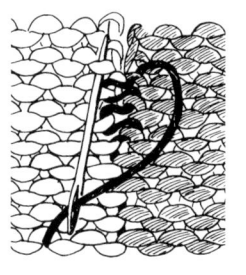

Work this seam from the right side of the knitting, placing the pieces to be seamed on a table, right sides up. Begin at the lower edge and work upward, row by row. Insert a threaded tapestry needle under the bottom loop of a purl stitch on one side of the seam, and then under the top loop of a corresponding purl stitch on the opposite side. Continue alternating from side to side, pulling the yarn in the direction of the seam, causing the loops from each side to merge and form a continuous row of purl bumps.

When the seam is complete, turn the work to the wrong side. Whipstitch (see page 87) once over the seam allowance to secure the seam, and then weave the tail end down through seam allowance for 2 inches (5 cm).

Invisible Weaving on Single (1 X 1) Rib

To get an uninterrupted single rib pattern across a seam, plan your ribbing with an odd number of stitches so that the first and last stitch on all right-side rows will be a knit stitch. Then for the best finishing results, treat the rib as stockinette stitch and work a one-half-stitch seam allowance (see page 72).

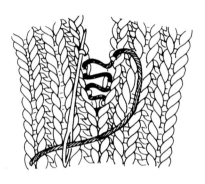

Work this seam from the right side. As with stockinette stitch, the edge knit stitches in ribbing alternate between loose and tight stitches. At the base of the V-shaped tighter stitches are horizontal bars. Alternating from side to side, catch these bars with the threaded tapestry needle and firmly pull together the two half stitches to form a whole knit stitch to make a smooth and continuous ribbing.

When the seam is complete, turn the work to the wrong side. Whipstitch (see page 87) once over the seam allowance to secure the seam, and then weave the tail end down through seam allowance for 2 inches (5 cm).

Invisible Weaving on Double (2 X 2) Rib

For an uninterrupted double rib pattern across a seam, the number of stitches in the ribbing must be a multiple of four plus two. The first two and last two stitches of a right-side row should be knit stitches. Treat the rib as stockinette stitch and work a one-stitch seam allowance (see page 73).

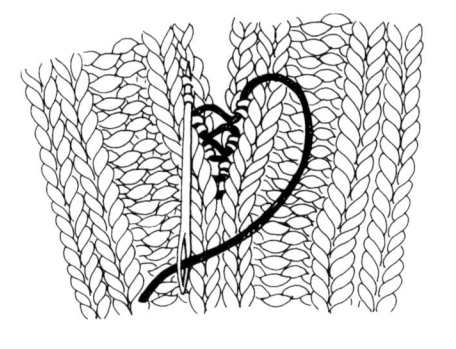

This seam is also worked from the right side. Between the first and second stitch from each edge, insert the threaded tapestry needle under two bars at a time, first on one side of the seam, and then on the other. This will create a stable seam and maintain well-shaped stitches.

When the seam is complete, turn the work to the wrong side. Whipstitch (see page 87) once over the seam allowance to secure the seam, and then weave the tail end down through seam allowance for 2 inches (5 cm).

Invisible Weaving on Garter Stitch

This seam is similar to the one used for reverse stockinette stitch (see page 74). Working from the right side, use a threaded tapestry needle to catch the bottom loop of the edge stitch on the knit ridge on one side of the seam, and then the top loop of the edge stitch on the knit ridge of the other side of the seam. When the seaming thread is pulled firmly, the loops from the two sides will merge to form a continuous knit ridge.

When the seam is complete, turn the work to the wrong side. Whipstitch (see page 87) once over the seam allowance to secure the seam, and then weave the tail end down through seam allowance for 2 inches (5 cm).

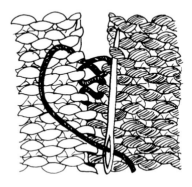

Seaming with Slip Stitch Crochet

This method is best for horizontal and curved seams such as shoulders and armholes. It will work for side and underarm sleeve seams as well, but produces more bulk in the seam allowance than you may want.

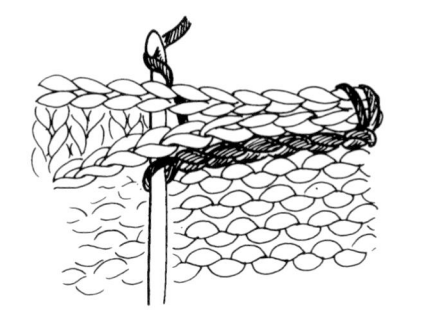

With right sides together and working one stitch at a time, insert a crochet hook through both thicknesses into the stitch just below the bound-off edge (or one stitch in from the selvedge edge). Catch the yarn and draw a loop through both thicknesses, then catch the yarn again and draw this loop through the first. This secures the end stitches together. *Insert the hook into the next stitch, through both thicknesses, and then catch and draw a loop back through both thicknesses and through the loop on the crochet hook; repeat from *, keeping the crochet stitches even.

To end, cut the yarn leaving a tail 6 to 8 inches (15 to 20 cm) long. Pull the tail end through the last stitch on the hook. Thread the tail on a tapestry needle and weave it back through the seam allowance for 2 inches (5 cm).

Slip stitch crocheted seams are easy to remove if you've made a mistake—just pull on the working yarn to ravel. Because it's so easily removed, it's ideal for experiments in placement or ease of seams. Of course, for those of you who crochet at the speed of light, this makes for quick finishing.

Backstitch Seaming

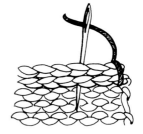

This strong seam is ideal for horizontal and curved seams such as shoulder and armhole edges. It creates slightly less seam bulk than slip stitch crochet and forms an elastic seam that allows for the easing in of fullness, as in a sleeve cap. The illustrations here show seaming the bound-off edges of shoulders.

Place right sides together and use a threaded tapestry needle to whipstitch (see page 87) the end stitches together. From the edge stitch, count over two stitches and insert a threaded tapestry needle directly under the bound-off stitches. Then count back one stitch and insert the needle under the bound-off stitches. Continue this circular motion—ahead two stitches from where the working yarn emerged from the previous stitch, and then back one stitch. Pull on the seam every few stitches to prevent the stitches from puckering.

For the most part, armholes consist of selvedge edges, not bound-off edges. However, armhole seams are worked as above with the threaded needle inserted right next to the selvedge. Always catch two strands of yarn, or a full stitch, for strength. As described above, move forward 1/2 inch (1 cm) and back 1/4 inch (0.5 cm).

Because the backstitch is somewhat difficult to remove, check the appearance on the right side frequently to avoid having to rip out the seam.

Invisible Horizontal Seam

This seam joins two bound-off edges, such as shoulder seams. It is similar to grafting, but is made by simply pulling the seaming yarn tight enough to cover the bound-off edges. The finished seam resembles a knit row. This seam requires that there be the same number of stitches on each bound-off edge.

Working from the right side with the bound-off edges lined up stitch for stitch, begin by inserting a threaded tapestry needle from back to front into the V of the stitch just below the bound-off edge. *Insert the needle under two strands of the knit stitch on the opposite piece, then under the next two strands of the first piece. Adjust the tension so that the seam looks like the knitted work; repeat from * to the end of the bound-off edge.

Invisible Vertical to Horizontal Seam

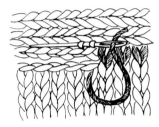

Use this method to join a bound-off edge to a selvedge edge, as in joining a sleeve to an armhole edge. Working from the right side, begin by bringing a threaded tapestry needle from back to front in the V of a knit stitch just below the bound-off edge. Insert the needle under one or two bars between the first and second stitch in from the selvedge edge, then insert the needle under two strands of a knit stitch just under the bound-off edge. Try to duplicate the tension of the knit stitch. Continue weaving back and forth between the two pieces until the seam is complete. Bring the needle to the wrong side of the work and secure the yarn in the seam.

Kitchener Stitch

The Kitchener stitch is used to graft together stitches so that the seam looks like a continuous row of stockinette stitch. Use this method to seam the toes of socks and underarms of sweaters that have been knit in the round.

Place the stitches to be grafted onto two needles and break the working yarn, leaving a tail roughly twice the length of the seam. Thread the tail of yarn onto a tapestry needle. Hold the two knitting needles together in the left hand with the needle points facing right and the wrong sides of the knitting facing together. Hold the threaded tapestry needle in the right hand. For best results, position the stitches near the points of the needles.

In preparation, use the tapestry needle to draw the working yarn through the first stitch on the front needle as if to purl, and leave it on the needle. Draw the yarn through the first stitch on the back needle as if to knit, and leave it on the needle. Then continue the seam as follows:

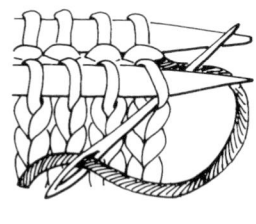

1. Draw the working yarn through the first stitch on the front needle as if to knit, and slip it off the needle.

2. Draw the yarn through the second stitch on the front needle as if to purl, but leave the stitch on the needle.

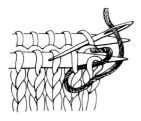

3. Draw the yarn through the first stitch on the back needle as if to purl, and slip it off.

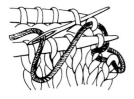

4. Draw the yarn through the second stitch on the back needle as if to knit, and leave the stitch on the needle.

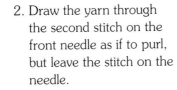

Repeat steps 1 through 4 until all stitches are joined. Strive to match the tension in the knitted work.

If you're unfamiliar with the Kitchener stitch, I heartily recommend knitting a pair of socks just to learn this technique. Besides, handknit socks are a delightful luxury.

Seaming a Vertical Border of Single (1 X 1) Rib

A border of ribbing that has been worked separately and sewn onto the front opening of a cardigan appears dressier than a ribbed border that was picked up from the opening and worked outward, although both techniques are equally stable in wear. The seam is most easily sewn if the ribbing is worked with a purl stitch on the edge to be seamed. The other edge will look most professional if the first stitch on the side that is not seamed is always slipped when it is at the beginning of the row.

Working from the right side, pin the border in place, stretching it slightly to prevent ripples. Thread a tapestry needle with matching yarn $1\frac{1}{2}$ times the length of the seam to be sewn. Insert the needle under the purl stitch bar that appears to bump outward at the edge on the ribbing side, under the bar 1/2 stitch in from the body edge, and into the tight-knit edge stitch. This 1/2-stitch seam allowance prevents the ribbing from bending outward, as can happen when a seam is too bulky. Continue to weave back and forth until border is completely sewn on.

HEMS AND HEMMING

Turning Rows

Hems are worked along the edges of garments that are designed to hang loosely from the body. The hem gives a neat finish and adds strength and firmness. Work the desired depth of hem facing, work one of the following turning rows to create a ridge that marks the hem foldline, and then work the body of the garment, securing the hem in place with the desired hem stitch (see pages 86–87).

SIMPLE TURNING RIDGE

Knit one row on the wrong side of the work to create a purl ridge on the right side of the work, which denotes the fold line.

PICOT

This forms a decorative and flexible turning row. The turning ridge is worked over an even number of stitches. On the right side: knit 1, *yarn over, knit 2 together; repeat from *, ending with k1.

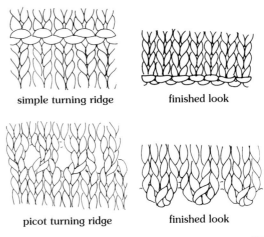

simple turning ridge   finished look

picot turning ridge   finished look

Hem Stitches

There are several ways to stitch a knitted hem in place. The most important consideration is that there be no visible line on the right side of the garment. For all methods, fold the hem to the wrong side along the turning ridge and pin it into place. Sew the hem in place with enough tension to secure it without causing it to pucker.

BACKSTITCH

The elastic quality of a backstitch is well suited for ribbings that are folded and stitched from the right side, such as neckbands or cuffs. It is worked with open stitches that have been placed on a contrasting color of yarn. The backstitch binds off the hem or band at the same time that it secures it in place.

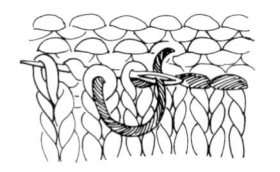

Work the backstitch as follows: remove the contrasting waste yarn to expose the open loops a few stitches at a time. Insert a threaded tapestry needle through an open loop, catching a stitch on the knitted body, then back through an open loop two stitches down and pull the yarn through. Count back one stitch and repeat.

WHIPSTITCH

Insert a threaded tapestry needle into a stitch on the wrong side of the knitting, and then into the cast-on edge of the hem. Moving from right to left, work stitch by stitch and repeat for the length of the hem.

whipstitch

KNIT-IN HEM

This type of hem requires no sewing. It may be used with a regular cast on as well as an invisible or open cast on. Work the hem and turning ridge of your choice. Then continue with the body of the piece until it is the same depth as the hem, ending with a wrong-side row. For a regular cast on, use a separate strand of yarn and an extra needle, and pick up one loop on the cast-on edge for each stitch on the main needle. Cut the extra yarn. (Alternately, use a smaller knitting needle and simply insert it into one half of the cast-on edge stitch as shown, thereby eliminating the need for extra yarn.) For an invisible cast on, clip out the waste yarn, placing each open loop on an extra needle. For both cases, fold up the hem so that wrong sides are together and the needles are held parallel to each other with the stitches for the main body held in front. Knit one stitch from the front needle together with one stitch from the back needle. Continue across row to secure the hem in place.

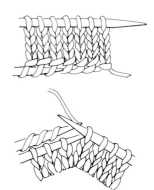

knit-in hem

BORDERS AND EDGES

Borders and finished edges give a garment stability and prevent the knitted pieces from curling. They need to be worked in stitches that lay flat, such as ribbing, garter, or seed stitch. In choosing a border, consider the finished look you desire. In general, the smoother the overall appearance of the border, the dressier the result. The more textural the border, the more casual the finished result. For example, a cardigan with a vertical single rib front border that has been worked separately and sewn on will give a dressy look to a cardigan. A front border that is picked up and worked in double rib will look more casual.

SINGLE (1 X 1) RIB

Worked on an even number of sts: knit 1, purl 1; repeat.

DOUBLE (2 X 2) RIB

Worked on a multiple of 4 sts: knit 2, purl 2; repeat.

single rib

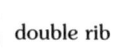

double rib

GARTER STITCH

Knit every row.

garter stitch

SEED STITCH

Worked on an even number of stitches:
Row 1: knit 1, purl 1.
Row 2: purl 1, knit 1.

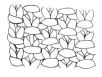

seed stitch

CROCHETED EDGES

Crocheted edges are usually narrower than knitted borders, and produce a subtle, clean finish. Single crochet and reverse single crochet, also called shrimp or crab stitch, are the most popular crocheted edges for knitted garments. Single crochet makes a smooth finish; reverse single crochet makes a decorative bead-like finish.

Single Crochet. Working from right to left, insert the crochet hook into a knit edge stitch, draw up a loop, bring the yarn over the hook, and draw this loop through the first one. *Insert the hook into the next knit stitch, draw up a loop, bring the yarn over the hook again, and draw this loop through both loops on the hook; repeat from * until the entire edge has been covered. Cut the yarn and secure the last loop by pulling the tail through it.

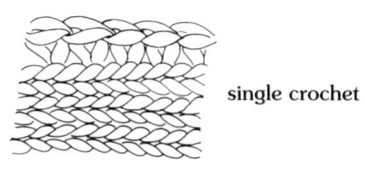

single crochet

Reverse Single Crochet (Shrimp Stitch or Crab Stitch). Working from left to right, insert the crochet hook into a knit edge stitch, draw up a loop, bring the yarn over the hook, and draw this loop through the first one. *Insert the hook into the next stitch to the right, draw up a loop, bring the yarn over the hook again, and draw this loop through both loops on the hook; repeat from * until the entire edge has been covered. Cut the yarn and secure the last loop by pulling the tail through it.

reverse single crochet

BUTTONHOLES

Eyelet Buttonhole

The eyelet buttonhole is self-sizing; bulky yarns make large holes that accommodate large buttons, fine yarns make small holes that accommodate small buttons. This buttonhole is virtually hidden in a border of single rib. Work the eyelet buttonhole on the right side as follows: yarnover, and then work the next two stitches together. That's all there is to it.

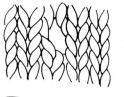

eyelet
buttonhole
in st st

eyelet
buttonhole
in single rib

Depending on the flexibility of the yarn and the stitch you have used, you may want to reinforce the buttonhole with overcasting or the buttonhole stitch.

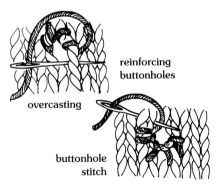

reinforcing
buttonholes

overcasting

buttonhole
stitch

One-Row Buttonhole

This visible horizontal buttonhole is neat and firm, and requires no reinforcing. The lower edge of the buttonhole is worked from the right side of the garment, and the upper edge is worked from the wrong side.

To work a one-row buttonhole, work to where you want the buttonhole to be, bring the yarn to the front, slip the next stitch purlwise, and then return the yarn to the back.

1. *Slip the next stitch and then on the right needle, pass the second stitch over the end stitch and drop it off the needle. Repeat from * three times. Slip the last bound-off stitch to the left needle and turn the work.

2. Move the yarn to the back and use the cable cast on to cast on five stitches as follows: *Insert the right needle between the first and second stitches on the left needle, draw up a loop, and place it on the left needle. Repeat from * four times. Turn the work.

3. With the yarn in back, slip the first stitch from the left needle and pass the extra cast-on stitch over it to close the buttonhole. Work to the end of the row.

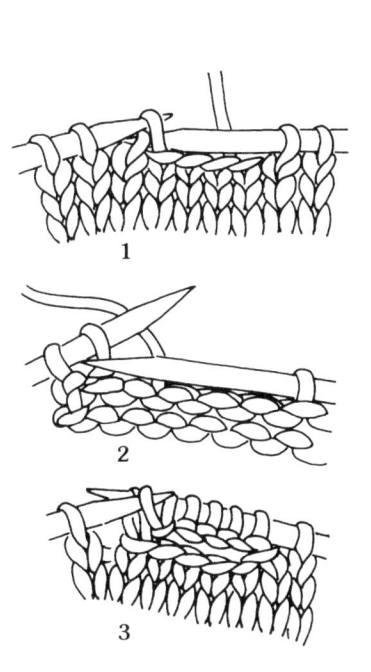

OTHER TECHNIQUES

Shortrowing

Shortrowing is a technique used to work partial rows, thereby increasing the number of rows in one area without having to bind off stitches in another; the number of stitches remains constant. This type of shaping eliminates the stairstep edges that occur when a series of stitches are bound off, as is common at the shoulders or neck. In shortrowing, you'll work across part of a row, turn the work, work back only part of the row, turn, etc. until the desired number of extra rows have been worked.

To prevent holes at the turning points, the slipped stitches are wrapped with the working yarn. Work the turning point of a knit row as follows:

1. With the yarn in back, slip the next stitch purlwise.

2. Pass the yarn between the needles to the front of the work.

3. Slip the same stitch back to the left needle and pass the yarn between the needles to the back of the work. Turn work.

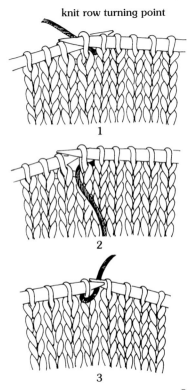

knit row turning point

1

2

3

Work the turning point of a purl row as follows:

1. With the yarn in front, slip the next stitch purlwise.

2. Pass the yarn between needles to the back of the work.

3. Slip the same stitch back to the left needle and pass the yarn back between the needles to the front of the work. Turn work.

After working the short rows, all of the stitches can be bound off at once, or they can be joined directly to another piece, as in binding off two shoulders together (see page 67), for a neat, flat, stable seam.

purl row turning point

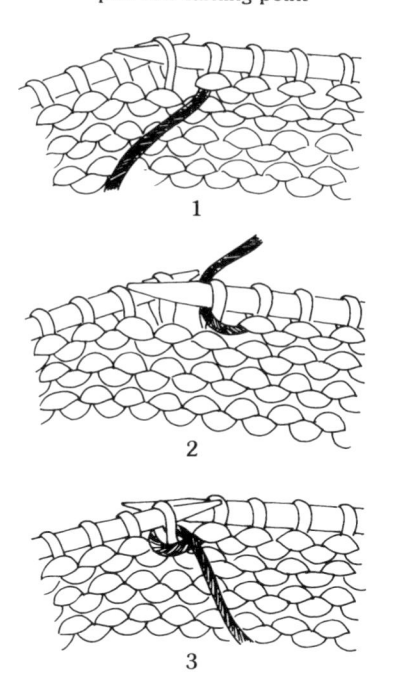

1

2

3

On the return rows, hide the wraps by working them together with the stitches that have been wrapped. On a knit row, work to just before the wrapped stitch, insert the right needle under the wrap and knitwise into the wrapped stitch, and knit them together as one.

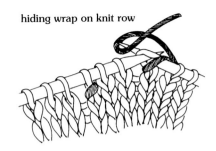

hiding wrap on knit row

On a purl row, work to just before the wrapped stitch, insert the right needle from behind into the back loop of the wrap, place the wrap on the left needle, and purl it together with the wrapped stitch on the left needle.

hiding wrap on purl row

Picking Up Stitches

S titches are picked up to create finished neckbands, cardigan borders, and pocket edges, and to work sleeves downward from the shoulders to the cuffs.

Always pick up stitches from the right side using a separate ball of yarn and a needle one or two sizes smaller than was used to knit the body of the garment (generally the size used for the ribbing). Beginning at the right corner of the edge to have stitches picked up, insert the needle under two strands of the selvedge or edge stitch, wrap the needle as if to knit, pull the loop through to right side, and leave the newly made stitch on the needle. Continue, working from right to left. Picked-up stitches can cause holes to form in the garment, especially along curved edges. Watch out for these and if you see one, take out that stitch and pick it up elsewhere. Continue until the desired number of stitches are on the needle.

An alternate method is to use a crochet hook to pick up the stitches, and then transfer them to a knitting needle every few stitches.

To make sure that the correct number of stitches are picked up evenly spaced, divide the knitted edge into fourths (or eighths for a very long edge) and mark these divisions with open markers. Then pick up one fourth (or eighth) of the desired total number of stitches in each section. (Note: the halfway point on a crew neckline that is open at one shoulder will not be at the shoulder seam.)

If you plan to use a stitch that has been used elsewhere in the garment, simply measure the gauge in that area. (Measure ribbing slightly stretched.) If you plan to use a new pattern, you will need to work a new 4-inch (10-cm) gauge sample. To compute the number of stitches to pick up, divide the length in inches (or cm) of the edge to be picked up by 4 and multiply this number by the number of stitches in your 4-inch (10-cm) gauge. For example, for a crew neckline that measures 25 inches (63.5 cm) long that is to have a ribbed neckband having a gauge of 18 stitches to 4 inches (10 cm), you would need to pick up about 112 stitches.

25 divided by 4 = 6.25 × 18 = 112.5

Round up or down as needed, remembering that a single rib requires an odd number of stitches and double rib requires a multiple of four plus two stitches when worked flat. (If you are knitting in the round, a single rib requires an even number of stitches; a double rib requires a multiple of four stitches.) Stockinette stitch can have any number of stitches.

Most patterns will tell you to "pick up and knit" a specific number of stitches. Read literally, this is somewhat misleading—you should not pick up a stitch and then knit it. You should pick up a stitch **as if to knit it,** and then leave it on the needle. When all stitches are on the needle, turn the work, and purl the next row for the neatest transition possible. With right side facing you again, begin the stitch pattern you plan to work for the border (or sleeves).

Color Knitting

K nitting with two or more colors of yarn produces exciting effects. Volumes have been written about color knitting. Seek them out for more information and inspiration. What's given here are the bare bones of the techniques for those who need a reminder and for those who need an introduction.

FAIR ISLE

F air Isle, or color stranding, is the technique of multi-colored knitting in which yarns that are not in use are carried loosely across the back of the work. In traditional Fair Isle, just two colors are used in a row, the colors are changed frequently, and diagonal pattern lines dominate over vertical lines to distribute the tension more evenly over the knitted fabric.

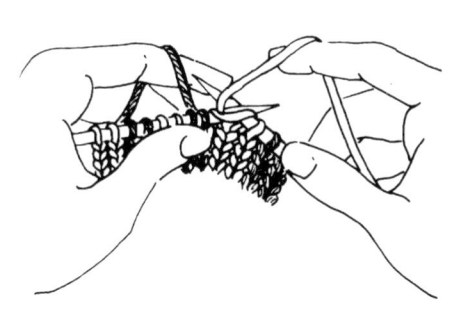

Fair Isle is worked most efficiently if the two yarns are held simultaneously; one in the left hand and worked in the Continental method (see pages 34-35), the other in the right hand and worked in the English method (see pages 36-37). Although this may feel awkward at first, it is well worth the effort because it allows for uniform stitches and rapid knitting.

You can prevent the two balls of yarn from tangling around each other as you knit by always stranding the right-hand yarn over the left-hand yarn and the left-hand yarn under the right-hand yarn. The wrong side of the work should be the mirror image of the front—do not twist the strands on the back.

In multicolor knitting, the stitches will pucker if the strands are pulled too tightly across the back, ruining the appearance. This can be prevented if you spread the stitches on the right-hand needle to their approximate gauge each time you change colors rather than allowing them to scrunch up near the tip of the needle.

In color knitting, you can keep track of the two yarns by always holding the pattern color in your right hand (English method) and always holding the background color in your left (Continental method). Use the English method to pass the yarn around the needle with your right hand, so that the working yarn passes over the background yarn on the back. Use the Continental method to pick the yarn held with your left hand, so that the working yarn passes under the pattern yarn on the back. If you work back and forth in rows, requiring that you strand as you purl, follow the same convention—pattern yarn strands over, background yarn strands under.

INTARSIA

Intarsia, or jacquard, is a method used to knit isolated blocks of color. These blocks may have vertical, horizontal, diagonal, or curved boundaries. Because the colors are used in limited areas, this type of knitting must be worked back and forth (knit one row, purl one row), not circularly. A separate "ball" of yarn is used for each color block. A little guess work is needed here—you'll have to estimate the amount of yarn that each block will require. For the technically adventurous, count the number of stitches in a block of color and then wind the yarn around the knitting needle that number of times to get a close estimate of yarn needed.

You can allow the strands of yarn to hang from the back or you can wind the yarn onto bobbins (a separate bobbin for each block). Tangles are inevitable, whether you use strands or bobbins, but it is often easier to pull single strands that are two to three armlengths or shorter through a tangle than to untangle bobbins. Let personal preference guide you.

Where the working yarns change, twist the yarns around one another to prevent holes in the knitting. Always pick up the new color from beneath the color that you had been working with. To change colors along a vertical line, twist the yarns around one another on every row. To change colors along a diagonal line, twist the yarns around one another on every other row. If the diagonal is right-slanting, twist the yarns only on the knit rows; if the diagonal is left-slanting, twist the yarns only on the purl rows. When working a right-slanting diagonal on the knit side, twist the yarns by bringing the new color over the top of the old one. On the following purl row, simply pick up the new color from under the old. When working a left-slanting diagonal on the purl side, twist the yarns by bringing the new color over the top of the old one.

READING CHARTS

Color charts are a visual guide to color or stitch motifs. Charts are usually presented on square graph paper with one square representing one stitch, even though knitted stitches are slightly wider than they are tall. Keep this in mind if you plan to design your own charted motifs—the knitted motif may appear shorter and wider than the charted design. Charts may be in color, or colors may be defined by different symbols. Unless otherwise noted, charts should be read from bottom to top. On right-side rows, read charts from right to left. On wrong-side rows, read charts from left to right. When knitting in the round, read charts from right to left for all rows.

You may find that the biggest challenge to reading a chart is keeping your place, especially if the chart is long and has many symbols. If you have trouble, consider placing the chart on a magnet board equipped with a magnetic straight edge (available from needlework shops). If you place the straight edge just above the row you are working on, you will be able follow the row you're working on as well as see the rows you have already completed, giving you a point of reference for subsequent color changes.

Using Double-Pointed Needles

Double-pointed needles, having points at both ends, come in sets of four or five in lengths of seven or ten inches. They allow you to knit smaller circumference pieces such as socks, mittens, sleeve cuffs, and neckbands circularly. When using double-pointed needles, the stitches are evenly divided between three needles, forming a triangle, and knit with the fourth, or divided between four needles, forming a square, and knit with the fifth. Cast on the required number of stitches on one needle, then divide the stitches evenly onto the others. Special care must be taken to avoid twisting the cast-on edge when the knitting is joined.

To join, lay the three needles in a triangle (or four needles in a square) on a flat surface. Arrange the cast-on edge so that it faces the inside of the triangle (or square). Keeping the needles in this arrangement, pick them up and use the fourth (or fifth) needle to begin knitting by inserting it into the very first cast-on stitch, and wrapping the needle with the working yarn which emerges from the last cast-on stitch.

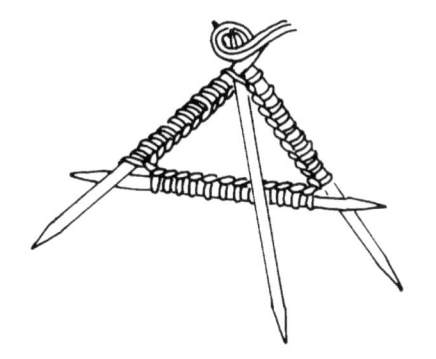

When joining double-pointed needles, the cast-on edge should face inside the triangle.

Tip: Hold the needles as illustrated, with needle 2 in the crook of your left hand, and needle 3 in the crook of your right hand.

Tip: To make a clean join, cast on using the long-tail method and work three or four stitches with both the working yarn and the tail end. Then drop the tail to be worked in later. The tail end will no longer be at the beginning of the round, so you will need to place an open marker in the knitting to define the beginning of the round.

Tip: To ensure a smooth transition in stitches from needle to needle with no loose stitches or visible vertical ridge, when knitting, bring the empty needle up from the bottom into the next stitch, as shown, so that it sits snugly against needle 3. Wrap the working yarn with some tension, but not so tightly that the yarn is stretched and the loft destroyed. When purling, bring the needle over needle 3 into the next stitch, as shown, and wrap the working yarn with some tension.

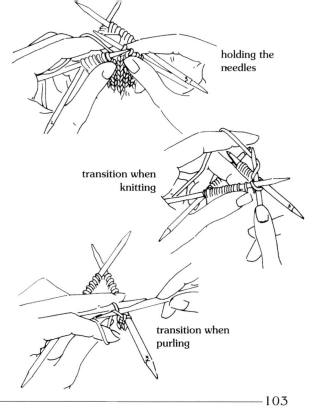

holding the needles

transition when knitting

transition when purling

Duplicate Stitch

This embroidery technique is used to cover knit stitches decoratively after the knitting is complete and the piece has been blocked. The duplicate stitch is worked with a tapestry needle threaded with yarn of the same weight or slightly heavier than the yarn used to knit the garment.

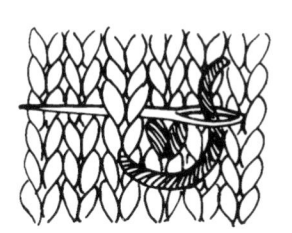

To work the duplicate stitch, bring the threaded tapestry needle up from the back at the base of the V of the knit stitch to be covered. Insert the needle under both loops of the stitch in the row above it, and pull the needle through. Insert the needle into the base of the V again, and pull the needle through to the back of the work.

Plain sweaters, both handknit and ready-made, can be enlivened with this easy embellishment. Choose one of the countless cross stitch and needlepoint charts to work from or get some graph paper and chart your own design. Keep in mind that knit stitches are slightly wider than they are tall, so designs charted on square graph paper will produce an image that appears compacted in height.

Correcting Errors

If you can recognize what knit and purl stitches should look like as they sit on the needles, you'll find that correcting errors is relatively simple. A correct knit or purl stitch forms an upside-down U over the needle. The right leg of the U falls in front of the needle and the left leg falls behind.

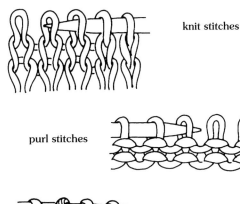

knit stitches

purl stitches

TWISTED STITCHES

A twisted or backward stitch will have the left side of the U in front of the needle. To correct it, simply use the other needle to lift the stitch off the needle, turn it around, and place it back on the needle with the right side of the U to the front.

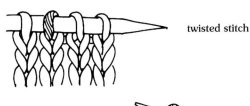

twisted stitch

correcting a
twisted stitch

DROPPED STITCHES

It is not uncommon to drop a stitch and for that stitch to ravel down one or more rows. You'll find a crochet hook helpful in picking up dropped stitches. Simply insert the hook, front to back, into the loop of the dropped stitch. Use the hook to catch the first horizontal "ladder" in the knitting and pull it through the loop to the front. Continue in this manner until all of the ladders have been used. Place the last loop on the needle, making sure that the right side of the U is on the front of the needle.

If a stitch drops and ravels on a purl row, you can simply turn the work around and correct as described above for the knit side, making sure to turn the work back around to finish the purl row. Or, you can pick up the dropped stitch from the purl side by inserting the crochet hook, back to front, into the loop of the dropped stitch, placing the

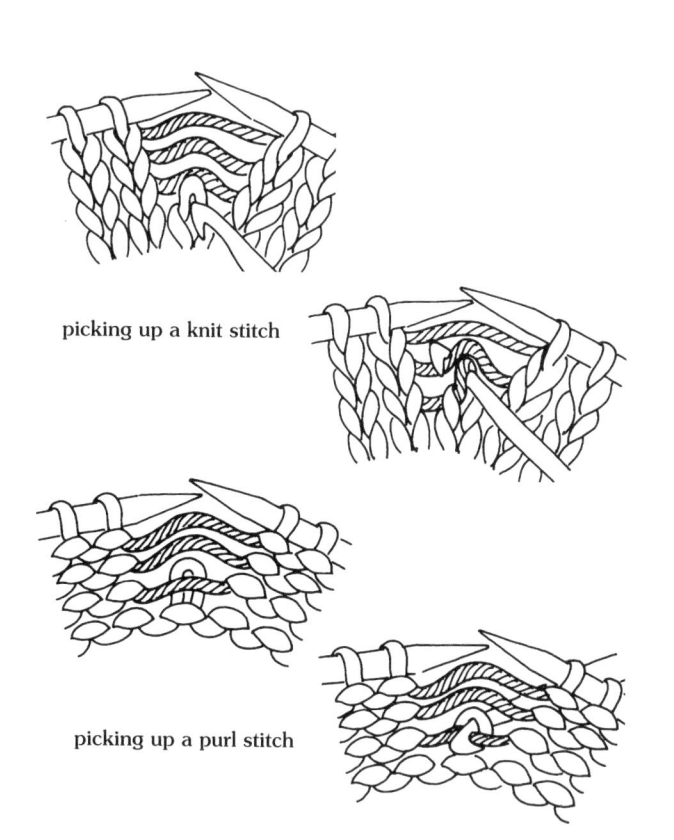

picking up a knit stitch

picking up a purl stitch

first horizontal "ladder" in front of the stitch, and pulling the ladder through the loop to the back. Continue in this manner until all of the ladders have been used. Place the last loop on the needle, making sure that the right side of the U is on the front of the needle.

When an edge stitch drops and ravels, there will be no visible "ladders" to chain up with a crochet hook. Instead, there will be a large loop extending from the edge above a small loop, below which the knitted edge is intact. To correct this error, insert the crochet hook into the small loop, and then, holding the large loop with some tension, pull the lower part of the large loop through the loop on the hook to form a stitch, then pull the upper part of the large loop through the loop on the hook to form a stitch, and finally catch the working yarn and pull it through the loop on hook. Place the last stitch on the needle. Edge stitches tend to look misshapen and this correction may make them even more so. But don't worry, they will be hidden in a seam.

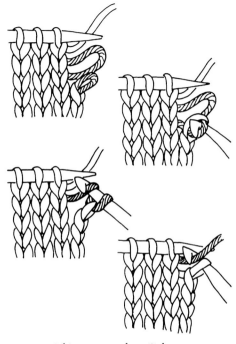

picking up an edge stitch

INCOMPLETE STITCHES

An incomplete stitch is a stitch from the previous row that is on the needle and the unworked strand of yarn either lies in a horizontal path across the back or is looped over the needle. If the unworked strand is in a horizontal path across the back, correct by using a crochet hook to pull the unworked strand through the stitch of the previous row, from the front for a knit stitch and from the back for a purl stitch. If the unworked strand is looped over the needle, correct by inserting the right knitting needle into the stitch of the previous row, and passing the stitch over the unworked strand. Then place the corrected loop on the needle so that the right side of the U is in front of the needle.

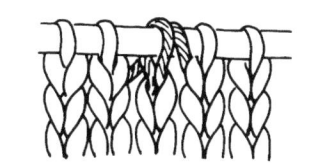

unworked strand on top of needle

use needle to pass stitch over unworked strand

TAKING OUT STITCHES

If you need to take out several stitches (up to a complete row) that have just been worked, simply "unknit" the stitches. Insert the left knitting needle into the front of the stitch in the row below the first stitch on the right needle for either a knit or purl stitch. Then, keeping the left needle in the stitch in the row below, pull on the working yarn as you ease the stitch off of the right needle and let it drop.

taking out a knit stitch

To pull out two or more rows, remove the needles from the stitches and pull on the working yarn to ravel the stitches to one row above the desired point. To prevent unwanted dropped stitches, pull out the last row, stitch by stitch, placing the open loops on a needle as you go. (These loops will be easier to place on a needle that is smaller than the one used to knit them—but be sure to change to the correct needle before you resume knitting.)

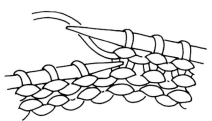

taking out a purl stitch

A FINAL WORD

There are people who treasure sweaters, and there are people who have not yet discovered their luxury. It is the knitter of those sweaters who enjoys magnified pleasure in the wearing of them. There is not a knitter alive who does not delight in a job well done and in wrapping up in a sumptuous knitted creation. Wearing a great sweater is like being hugged by your best friend all day.

Great sweaters are knitted with great technique. I believe in developing a firm foundation of solid, flawless technical ability. When the physical logistics of technique are no longer a stumbling block, creativity can flow in an abundant stream of delightful experience. The door to what you may accomplish is thrown wide open.

INDEX

abbreviations 29–31
axis stitch 56
bind offs 65–67; basic 65; binding off together 67; loose bind-off loop 66; sloped or bias 66
blocking 68–69
body measurements, tables of 20–24; taking 18–19
borders and edges 88–90; crocheted 89–90; garter stitch 89; rib stitches 88; seed stitch 89
buttonholes 91–92; eyelet 91; one-row 92; reinforced 91
cast ons 41–46; cable 43; invisible 46; long-tail 44–45; needle size to use 41; number of stitches 41; open/openwork 40, 46, 57, 58; temporary 46
charts, reading 101
color knitting 98–101; Fair Isle 98–99; intarsia 100; reading charts 101
color stranding *see Fair Isle*
colorfastness, test for 12
Continental method of knitting 34–35
conversions; crochet hooks 28; knitting needles 27; weights and lengths 26
crochet hook conversions 28

crochet, stitches 89–90; in seaming 78
decreases 59–64; double 61, 63; knit two together 59; left-slanting 60, 61, 62; purl two together 62; right-slanting 59, 62, 63; slip knit pass 61; slip purl pass 63; slip slip knit 60; vertical double 64
double pointed needles, using 102–103
duplicate stitch 104
ease allowance for sweaters 25
English method of knitting 36–37
errors, correcting 105–109; dropped stitches 106–107; incomplete stitches 108; taking out stitches 109; twisted stitches 105
Fair Isle 98–99
felting, avoiding 12
gauge 32–33
handwashing 12–13
hem stitches 86–87
hems and hemming 85–87; turning rows 85
increases 50–58; bar 51, 56; double 56–57; keeping track of 50; left-slanting 55; make one, left slant 55, 57; make one, right slant 54, 57; open/openwork 40, 46, 57, 58; placement of 50; raised 52–53, 57; right-slanting 54

intarsia 100

jacquard *see intarsia*

joining yarns 47–49; at the side edge 47; by overlapping yarns 48; by splicing 49

knit stitch; Continental method 34; English method 36

knitting needle conversions 27

measuring knitted pieces 38

"pick up and knit" 97

picking up stitches 96–97

purl stitch; Continental method 35; English method 37

seaming 70–84; backstitch 79; garter stitch 77; how to begin 71; invisible horizontal 80; invisible vertical to horizontal 81; kitchener stitch 82–83; reverse stockinette stitch 74; rib 75, 76, 84; slip stitch crochet 78; stockinette stitch 72, 73

shortrowing 93–95

slip knot 42

slipping stitches 39

stitches, axis 56; backstitch 79, 86; dropped 106–107; duplicate 104; garter 89; hem 86–87; incomplete 108; kitchener 82–83; knit-in hem 87; reverse single crochet 90; rib 88; seed 89; single crochet 90; slipping 39; taking out 109; twisted 105; yarnover 40; whipstitch 87

storing garments 13

supplies 6

sweaters, ease allowance 25; yardage estimates for 16–17

symbols, yarn label 10–11

tension *see gauge*

washing, by hand 12–13

yardage (meter) estimates for sweaters 16–17

yarn, formula for interchanging 14–15; label symbols 10–11; sizes 8–9; structure 7

yarnover 40